Interpol

PETER G. LEE

Interpol

STEIN AND DAY/*Publishers*/New York

First published in 1976
Copyright © 1976 by Peter G. Lee
All rights reserved
Designed by Ed Kaplin
Printed in the United States of America
Stein and Day/*Publishers*/Scarborough House,
Briarcliff Manor, N.Y. 10510

Library of Congress Cataloging in Publication Data

Lee, Peter G
    Interpol.

    1.   International Criminal Police Organization.
2. Criminal investigation.   I. Title.
HV7240.L43   364.12'06'21   75-34292
ISBN O-8128-1906-3

To Françoise

ACKNOWLEDGEMENTS

It would be impossible to thank all the people in the General Secretariat of Interpol who spent their time with me answering questions and providing me with details about the various cases described in this book.

However, I would like especially to thank the three department heads of the criminal sections of the General Secretariat: Police Commissaire Serge Langlais, Detective-Superintendent Raymond Kendall, and Police Commissaire Michel Mikkleson. They were more than generous with their time and information. Certainly without their help and knowledge this book could not have been written.

Foreword

Although the name Interpol is well known throughout the world, very few people know exactly what Interpol is or how it functions. This book was written to show, in part, what work Interpol does as well as to illustrate some of the types of cases it helps to solve.

The material for this book was researched at the headquarters of Interpol, the General Secretariat, located in St. Cloud, France. Information about the criminal cases was supplied by records on file as well as by many hours of verbal sessions with various Interpol staff members.

The importance of Interpol's work in the field of international police cooperation and in exploiting new techniques for fighting crime is self-evident. I sincerely hope this book emphasizes that importance.

Chapter 1

The well-dressed man didn't attract much attention when he passed through immigration at Osaka International Airport. He'd arrived a few minutes earlier on Singapore Airlines Flight SQ 632, from Bangkok. The plane had been ten minutes late, touching down at exactly 7:50 P.M.

If his manner appeared a little anxious, a bit nervous, it could have been attributed to his halting use of the Japanese language. He had to be asked twice by the immigration officer how long he planned to stay in Japan. As a matter of fact, he spoke Japanese perfectly.

His passport showed him to be a Thai national named Anant Bongsang. He explained that he was on a sightseeing trip and expected to stay for one week.

He got through customs quickly, his one bag drawing only a cursory examination from the official on duty. Once outside the terminal building, he placed his suitcase next to his feet so that a large blue Pan American Airways sticker was prominently displayed toward the cars moving in to pick up arriving passengers.

Within seconds, a light-green Datsun sedan pulled up in front of him. The driver leaned across the front seat and through the open window on the passenger side asked if he was Anant Bongsang.

Bongsang admitted his name and, picking up his suitcase, immediately got into the back of the Datsun. As the car swung into the departing airport traffic, he relaxed against the back of the seat and patted the jacket of his hand-tailored Italian suit, feeling the bulge of the envelope in the inside pocket. The envelope contained one million yen. Later, through the black market, he would exchange it for three thousand American dollars. He was much more concerned, however, with the rendezvous he had come to Osaka to keep. If things went well for him at the meeting, he would close a deal that would make three thousand dollars seem like a pauper's dowry.

.

At the same time that Anant Bongsang was riding toward his appointment, a black Mercedes sedan slid smoothly to a stop in front of a night club known as the Locust. The driver of the car, a large Korean named Pak Yung Wan, worked for the man in the back seat, Inaba Kondo, a Japanese businessman.

Kondo met the eyes of his driver in the mirror. "Are we having any problems with the new group?" He spoke in a characteristically crisp manner, snapping out the words.

"You'll have to speak to them. There's one in particular. She's raising objections, and the others are listening to her."

"Then they haven't gone to work yet?"

"No, they're still in their rooms."

Inaba Kondo owned the Locust Club. It was a private club open only to members and their guests. Nonmembers who wanted to spend an evening there had to pay an enrollment fee at the door. The minimum eating and drinking charge was ten thousand yen. For visiting Americans that translated to thirty-five dollars.

Every customer who stayed in the club had to select a hostess as his companion for the evening. Her fee was thirty thousand yen per hour. The customer also had to pay an additional fifty thousand yen for her services in his bed, whether he used this service or not.

Kondo had become a rich man in the three years he had run the Locust. He exercised iron control over his hostesses, whom he recruited exclusively from Thailand. His wife, Shinko, was the madam of the club and handled all the financial arrangements with the customers.

Kondo prided himself on the fact that his girls were the youngest and prettiest in the city of Osaka. He had a man in Bangkok who supplied him with a never-ending stream of girls. The man in Bangkok was Anant Bongsang, a petty crook and sometime pimp. Kondo paid him forty thousand yen for each girl. They had met in Bangkok when Kondo had visited that city to look for a source for girls.

He had found Bongsang to be prompt in his service, selective in his choice of girls, and, more important, satisfied with the financial arrangement. He knew that if Bongsang ever saw the Locust Club operation, he would demand a lot more money. Happily, Bongsang had never visited Japan and, as far as Kondo knew, had no intentions of doing so.

Once in a while, a troublesome girl would show up in the group. He was always warning Bongsang to make sure of the girls before putting them on the plane. Actually, Kondo wasn't too alarmed if one of the girls objected to becoming a prostitute. It gave him a chance to make an example of her for the benefit of the others.

Officially, the club was open from seven in the evening until two in the morning. In practice, most people left at midnight, for it was at that hour that the girls were permitted to go with the customers. Kondo wanted the girls on the premises until twelve so that he could collect the hourly charge for their companionship at the tables.

Inaba Kondo got out of the Mercedes and, followed by his driver, Pak, went inside the club. The interior was spacious, partitioned to make it appear circular. Tiny booths for two were bunched against the walls, separated by thin screens. Tables and chairs crowded in toward a small dance floor, taking up the rest of the free space.

As the club had opened for business about an hour earlier, the orchestra was already playing, and a few of the tables had customers at them, attended by Kondo's hostesses.

Kondo walked to the rear of the club to his private office. Pak followed, stopping at the door. Kondo motioned him inside, then locked the door.

He sat down at his desk and pressed a button located next to the top drawer. At once the paneled wall at the back of the office slid open to reveal another entrance.

"Bring them all up here, Pak," Kondo ordered.

Pak went through the entrance, and his footsteps could be heard padding softly down a flight of carpeted stairs.

While waiting for Pak's return, Kondo selected a long thin

cigar from an enameled cigar box resting on his desk. He used a little gold knife to clip off the end, then lighted up and waited.

A rustle of movement could be heard on the stairs. Five girls came into the office, followed by Pak and Kondo's wife, Shinko. The girls were wearing the semitransparent long gowns provided by the club.

They were young and beautiful. Bongsang had said that in this group not one girl was older than twenty-two. If he had been remiss in selecting them for their cooperative spirit, he had certainly taken pains in selecting them for their looks. Kondo studied them, trying to guess which one might be the troublemaker. He knew from experience that one like that could sour the rest.

He introduced himself and gave them the short speech he always gave to the new girls: "Welcome to the Locust Club. I hope you had a good flight from Bangkok and that you aren't too tired because you'll be starting work tonight." He spoke in Thai, easily and fluently.

The girls had arrived in Osaka at five-thirty that same afternoon, on Korean Airways Flight KE 504. Kondo's wife had met them at the airport and brought them straight to the Locust. From now on they would be living in the basement sleeping quarters underneath the club.

Two men entered the office from the stairway. These two, Imai Kunishiro and Sakurai Norio, were known to the Osaka Police for their activities as enforcers for various racketeer groups. They had been working for Kondo for the past year. He used them to maintain order and discipline among the girls in their quarters, like harem guards. They moved near Pak and Shinko and stood quietly.

Kondo went on speaking to the girls. He pointed to his wife. "You've already met my wife and I'm sure she explained your duties here but I'll go over them again for you. You'll be joining my other hostesses in the club, working seven days a week. We supply you with a place to sleep, your food, your gowns, just as you were told we would before you left Bangkok. Think of the Locust Club as your home.

"We pay a good percentage to you on the drinks your customers order and a nice percentage for the services you provide for them outside the club. The hotel you'll use for this is mine and is near here. In the mornings you'll be escorted from the hotel back to your quarters. My wife is in charge inside the club, and all the financial arrangements will be handled by her." He waited to see if the girls had anything to say, but they remained silent, watching him.

"For each all night date with a customer, you'll receive ten thousand yen. We settle up with you once a month, deducting a fair amount for your room and board and clothing. Now, do any of you have a question?"

A very short, slim girl, who appeared to be the youngest of the group, took a tentative step forward. Shinko identified her to Kondo as Patma Vanee.

Patma looked very frightened and had difficulty speaking. "In Bangkok, none of us were told about servicing customers outside the club. This work was represented to me as strictly a hostess job." She began to cry.

Kondo smiled at her. "Come here," he said kindly.

She approached his desk gingerly. He took one of her hands between both of his, then gently stroked her hand. "You have beautiful hands and fingers," he told her.

He stopped stroking her hand and closed his fist around her index finger. "Lovely, lovely, slim fingers," he said.

His hand wrenched up suddenly, not letting go of her finger. There was a snapping sound as the finger broke, the bone darting up through the skin at the knuckle joint.

She screamed and tried to tear free of him. He held her close and without hurrying broke the finger next to the index finger in the same way. She started to fall, like a floppy rag doll, when he released her.

The big Korean, Pak, stepped in quickly and caught her, then lowered her to the floor. She lay there sobbing, curling herself into a little ball.

Kondo looked at the other girls. They were in various stages of shock. "As you must know, this is a business," he explained. "For any business to operate smoothly, there must be complete understanding between employer and employees."

The girls had huddled together as if to gain strength from each other. Their eyes were fixed on the girl on the floor.

"I understand," Kondo continued, "others of you have some objections to working here. Is that so?"

There was no answer.

"Good. Just to show you that we're serious about our dealings with our employees, we'll give you a chance to see what can happen to any one of you who gives us trouble." He nodded to Pak and the two other men.

The Korean's wide, flat face split into a grin. He reached down to the girl on the floor and slapped her lightly across the face. She made a move to roll away from him, but the other two men grabbed her shoulders and pinned her to the carpet.

Pak yanked at the front of her gown and the flimsy material tore apart, leaving her in her undergarments. She was unable to move, but her eyes bulged from their sockets as Pak took off the rest of her clothing.

At this point, with the girl Patma Vanee naked and securely held down by the men, Pak paused to look at Kondo.

Kondo nodded his head.

The three men then took turns raping the girl in front of their frightened and horrified audience. When they finished, Pak picked up the now unconscious girl and threw her onto a couch.

Kondo stared at the other girls. He looked them over slowly, then pointed at one of them. His wife, Shinko, promptly identified her as Binjad Kasorn.

"You," Kondo said. "Do you have any problems?"

She could only shake her head in response. She was too terrified to speak.

Kondo signaled Pak. The Korean took her by the nape of her neck and pushed her roughly forward toward the desk. She twisted helplessly in his grip, her eyes on Kondo.

"I think you might cause some trouble," Kondo told her.

She shook her head negatively.

"Are you absolutely certain?"

14

"Yes," she managed to say.

"Let her go," Kondo instructed. "In fact," he went on, "all of you may now go downstairs to your quarters. My wife will give you some brief instructions so you can begin your work. You have a long night ahead of you."

When the four men were left in the room with the unconscious girl, Kondo jerked a thumb in her direction. "Get rid of her," he ordered.

•

In another part of the city, Anant Bongsang was deep in conversation with a man known as Trader Willy. This was the man Bongsang had flown almost three thousand miles to see. Trader Willy's real name was Toshio Harada. He was a man of many business interests. In fact, the bar they were using for a meeting place was called Willy's, after its owner. His nickname had been given him by countless American soldiers during the Korean war. The Americans were gone now but the name remained.

To policemen Willy was a well-known character. His arrest record dated back twenty-five years. But in spite of all the arrests there had been very few convictions. Willy was a careful operator, extremely discreet in all his affairs. He had never spent time in jail. All of his arrests had been for minor offenses. Now, however, he was preparing to take a step in a dangerous direction.

For a long time he had watched Inaba Kondo piling up money. He knew Kondo's activities were not confined to the Locust Club. Willy was one of the few people not working with Kondo who knew that Kondo was the biggest supplier of forced prostitutes in Japan. Girls coming into the country were filtered through the Locust Club to other cities, and on each girl Kondo knocked down a handsome profit. Painstakingly, through his own contacts, Willy had found out that Bongsang was Kondo's supplier.

When Willy decided to compete with Kondo, he found an eager accomplice in Bongsang. Both of them were careful to keep their meeting a secret. Kondo had powerful underworld connections that could end their partnership abruptly.

Anant Bongsang, after seeing the girls board the Korean Airways flight at 9:10 A.M. in Bangkok, had phoned Kondo in Osaka to tell him they were on the way. Kondo had no way of knowing that Bongsang had then boarded the 11:20 A.M. Singapore Airlines flight to get to Osaka some two and a half hours after the girls.

Bongsang and Willy had agreed that Willy would make an initial purchase of ten girls at a cost of 2.7 million yen. This was a delivered price, F.O.B. Osaka International Airport. Payment was to be in American money, roughly nine thousand dollars.

It was further agreed that Willy would purchase another ten girls each month at the same price. Bongsang was offering no discounts, despite Willy's argument that his volume of business deserved a price break.

Once more, Bongsang went over his procurement methods. He explained how his advertisements for work in Japan's big-city night clubs lured the girls. They were promised food and lodging and plane fare to their destination. Prostitution was never discussed. When the girls finally found out what they were hired for, Bongsang pointed out, there was not much they could do about it. For the few who raised strenuous objections, there were ways and means of making them come around.

Now that the deal was firmed up, Bongsang asked Willy to get his money for him. Willy suggested waiting a day, but Bongsang insisted on being paid immediately. Willy sent out a man for the money and proposed that the new partners have a drink in the meantime.

It was unfortunate Bongsang chose to get his money so quickly. If he'd waited another day, things might have worked out differently.

The man who had gone to get the money was a suspected opium dealer. He was the same man who had picked up Bongsang at the airport, a Korean national named Sang Lee Kim.

Kim didn't know it, but he was under constant surveillance by the Osaka Police. When he climbed into the green Datsun and started the motor, a detective in an unmarked police car started his own motor and prepared to follow Kim.

The detective, Toyo Koisi, was not especially interested in Kim's business with Trader Willy. However, he had noticed that the well-dressed man whom he thought was a Thai was still in the bar when Kim left. He used his car radio to ask that someone intercept this Thai and get some positive identification from him. He felt it might develop into something.

About an hour later, as Anant Bongsang left the bar with his money, he was stopped in the street by a detective who asked him to identify himself. Unafraid, Bongsang produced his passport. After jotting down the facts in the passport, the detective offered some excuses about making a mistake and walked away. Bongsang continued on foot to his hotel nearby.

The detective relayed the information on Bongsang to his lieutenant, and after a short discussion with Toyo Koisi, a call was made to Tokyo. It was made to the Criminal Research and Statistics Division, Criminal Investigation Bureau, National Police Agency. That cumbersome title was the official name of Interpol-Japan.

Chapter **2**

The organization known to the world as Interpol has sometimes been described as an outfit of chisel-jawed, gimlet-eyed crime fighters who put their lives in jeopardy every working hour.

Less flatteringly, Interpol has also been described as a huge filing cabinet, stuffed with clerks choking on their own statistics.

As with most generalities, there is some truth in both statements. There are, certainly, some grim battlers of crime to be found working with Interpol. There are, just as surely, those drones shuffling mountains of paper whose cheeks are sallow from their indoor life.

Consider the charisma of the name alone: INTERPOL. Interpol, the international police force. Continents leaped in a single bound, oceans crossed in the space of a breath! Villains watched by eyes that never sleep. Surprisingly, a lot of it happens almost that way.

The Interpol story begins in 1914, a few months before the world went to war, when a meeting was held in Monaco at the invitation of Prince Albert I to discuss better methods of fighting international crime. The meeting was attended by representatives of fourteen countries and territories. They called themselves the First International Criminal Police Congress. The major topics discussed were unification of extradition laws, maintenance of central files on criminals, better identification methods, and simpler and faster arrests. The proceedings were highly praised by the local press.

Just when it seemed that the participants would be able to put something viable together, the war began. Their ideas had to wait for more peaceful times.

In September, 1923, in Vienna, another conference was

held, called the Second International Criminal Police Congress. At this time a permanent body for police cooperation was created. It was to be named the International Criminal Police Commission (I.C.P.C.) and to be headquartered in Vienna.

The I.C.P.C. developed gradually until 1938, when thirty-four nations claimed membership. But in March of that year, when Hitler gobbled up Austria, for all practical purposes the I.C.P.C. ceased to function. Its headquarters were moved to Berlin, and that was that.

In 1946, with the war over, a congress was held in Brussels to revive the I.C.P.C. Seventeen nations were represented. A new constitution was formed and an executive committee of five members elected. The commission's headquarters were moved to Paris. A telegraph address was necessary and the word Interpol, a contraction of "international police," was chosen and registered on July 22, 1946. The press was delighted with this new word and began referring to the organization simply as Interpol.

In 1956, when the constitution was again revised and the name was changed from the unwieldy International Criminal Police Commission to the equally unwieldy if slightly different International Criminal Police Organization-Interpol, the word Interpol was officially sanctioned. Since then, of course, most of the world has used only the name Interpol, and it's a winning bet that few people can remember the mouthful that precedes it.

In 1966, Interpol moved again but not very far. This time it was to a spanking-new building in the Paris suburb of St. Cloud.

Interpol is funded by its member nations. Before 1956, contributions were calculated on the basis of a country's population. Since 1957, the Interpol General Assembly has made up a scale of budget units, each one worth 4,850 Swiss francs. When a country joins Interpol it selects the amount it feels it wants to pay to the organization.

Four groups coordinate and direct the activities of Interpol. They are the General Assembly, the Executive Commit-

19

tee, the General Secretariat, and the National Central Bureaus.

The General Assembly and the Executive Committee are made up of delegates from member nations. Their function is to meet periodically and make the decisions about the overall operation of Interpol. The General Assembly is the supreme authority. It elects the Executive Committee, which is composed of thirteen members including the president, three vice-presidents, and nine delegates. The Executive Committee normally meets twice a year.

The day-to-day working machinery is run by the other two groups, the General Secretariat and the National Central Bureaus. These are the permanent, visible components of Interpol.

The General Secretariat is not responsible to any single government. It accepts authority only from I.C.P.O.-Interpol. This way it preserves an international character. It consists of a Secretary General, the chief full-time official of Interpol, and a technical and administrative staff. As outlined in the constitution of Interpol, the General Secretariat is responsible for carrying out the orders and decisions of the General Assembly and the Executive Committee. It serves as an international center in the fight against crime and as an information and technical center. It maintains contact with its member nations and their police authorities.

The National Central Bureaus, or NCBs, are those bodies designated by the member nations to serve as their link with Interpol. These are the front-line troops, the action people. In the United States, the Treasury Department is the National Central Bureau. In the United Kingdom, it's Scotland Yard; the Questore in Italy; the Melbourne City Police in Australia; and the Sureté in France.

Because police organization varies from country to country the NCBs were established to act as the one special group to handle Interpol chores and ensure maximum cooperation between nations. Each NCB is usually an official government body with police powers. If a country has only one central police authority, that body becomes the National Central

Bureau. Of course, any service appointed as an NCB is bound to its nation's laws and authority and retains its national title.

The basic effectiveness of Interpol depends upon the actions of the NCBs. They are the ones to get help from other services in their country, and the speed with which they transmit information to member nations determines the excellence of Interpol as a whole.

What this cooperation means was shown in the case of an assistant bank manager in Japan who stole several million dollars. He had worked with an accomplice, a company director who submitted forged bills to the bank which the assistant manager accepted. Both men dropped out of sight before the police could make an arrest. By means of circulating their photographs and arrest warrants to all Interpol member nations, it was possible to apprehend the pair. One was arrested in Hong Kong, the other three days later in Paris. Almost all the stolen money was recovered.

Each NCB is connected by radio to the regional station for its geographic zone. The regional stations are connected to the Central Station in France. This radio network is versatile. Network stations can monitor the Central Station or any regional station. Because of this, messages can be broadcast to more than one station at a time. A coding system determines the urgency of each message so that those with high priority can be given precedence.

Interpol uses other communication tools as well. Radioteleprinters and phototelegraphy equipment permit rapid transfers of fingerprints and photographs. Sometimes even more advanced technology is employed. When the police all over the world were looking for a Canadian named George Leray, they turned to the Early Bird Satellite. Leray had led his gang on a daring holdup of a Montreal bank and gotten away with $4 million. Scotland Yard broadcast Leray's photograph to the world by satellite. An American who saw the picture in Florida recognized Leray as a man who was living on a yacht in Fort Lauderdale under an assumed name. The police were alerted and arrested Leray.

One of the single biggest jobs done at the General

Secretariat in St. Cloud is record keeping. Because Interpol understood that no police service is effective without comprehensive records, they set up a special Criminal Records Department. This department has two aims. One is to gather as much information as it can about international criminals and the offenses they commit and to classify and update this information. The other is to identify offenders and their methods of operation.

The criminal records are divided into two headings: general and specialized.

The general records contain all the information that floods the General Secretariat each day concerning criminals and their activities. This includes such things as fingerprints, investigation reports, drug seizure forms, telegrams, photographs, and copies of correspondence between the NCBs. These items come in at the rate of a thousand a day.

All these items must be analyzed at once and the proper files searched and brought up to date for the specialized groups. This work is organized in three indexes. The first consists of names and aliases, nicknames, and family names. There are over a million and a half cards in this index. The second index comprises all legal identity documents, such as identity cards and passports. Registration numbers of firearms and cars are also kept in this index. The third index is reserved for records of actual offenses, classified as to type and when and where committed.

There is another record group, containing individual files, case files, and reference folders. The individual files compile information about a particular individual so that his criminal career is kept current. The reference folders keep track of correspondence exchanged by the NCBs without an official notification to the General Secretariat. The case files are filled with documents implicating more than one person in a criminal case.

The specialized records section is concerned with the identification of criminals. There are three indexes used; the ten-print index, the single-print index, and the photographic index.

The ten-print index is the traditional type of fingerprint card, carrying fingerprints of the criminal, his identity and file number. These cards come in from the various NCBs.

The single-print index is also traditional but only criminals who may leave prints at the scene of a crime are catalogued. This index is made up of known murderers and burglars.

The photographic index is just what its name implies. It is used when no fingerprints are available. To simplify use of this index, the cards are arranged according to the different methods used by the criminals. Within each of these groups, the photographs are classified by a formula based on Bertillon's *portrait parlé* system.

The full usefulness of these indexes is evident in the case of a man known as a swindler and trafficker in arms and wanted for fraud in Chad, Africa. An international notice was sent out after an arrest warrant was issued by a court in Chad. The wanted man had opened an investment company in the Bahamas and signed contracts for a hotel chain to be built in Chad. Through fraud he raised the money for hotels he never constructed.

The General Secretariat was soon able to inform Chad that the man had been arrested in Switzerland and extradited to West Germany for another series of frauds committed there. Canada and the United Kingdom then reported that the man was also suspected of fraud in their countries. The authorities in all these places knew the man was the one they wanted, thanks to the identification procedures of the General Secretariat. Each member nation had received the international notices on the suspect.

The working staff of the General Secretariat is made up of police officers and civilians. The police officers come from the member nations and are assigned by them to work in the St. Cloud headquarters. Most of them are bilingual or trilingual and are experts in certain fields. Each police officer works in one of three departments associated with different types of crimes. One group concentrates on thefts and crimes of violence. Another works with narcotics. The third works with crimes such as counterfeiting, forgery, and swindles.

As part of the vital police work of identification, the General Secretariat assumes as one of its responsibilities the circulation of the international notices. These notices are constantly updated and are published in the three official working languages of Interpol: English, French, and Spanish. They are classified into four types, distinguished as to type by color.

The notices coded red are issued to arrest a suspect for purposes of extradition. The red notice is very exact about the type of warrant involved, enabling the police to make a quick arrest. This international circulation of arrest warrants is an idea that became a reality solely through the efforts of Interpol. These documents permit provisional arrest.

The notices coded green are warning notices. They alert police that the person described in the notice is a professional international criminal.

Blue notices are circulated for the purpose of collecting more information about the person named. The aim is to check his identity, get a list of his prior crimes and convictions, or to get a last address.

The fourth notice is coded black. These notices are used to establish the identity of a corpse.

The General Secretariat also issues stolen-property notices, letters, summary reports, and technical brochures. Circular letters are used to transmit various information about criminal devices, modus operandi, and movements of criminals.

It was thanks to a circular that a ring of gold smugglers was broken. The circular described what was then a unique way of transporting gold illegally across a country's frontier. The gold was hidden in a special vest that could be worn under other garments. A criminal using one of these vests could carry as much as eighty pounds of the metal in one smuggling trip.

Interpol has been growing steadily. As of the first of January 1975, there were 120 member nations.

Interpol's aims and actions are regulated by its constitution. Its goals are to provide and promote assistance among all criminal police authorities under the laws of each nation and to help all institutions that can act effectively in the cause of prevention and suppression of crime. I.C.P.O.-Interpol is forbidden to become involved in any activities of a military, political, religious, or racial nature.

•

When the police in Osaka placed that call to the NCB of Japan in Tokyo, several things happened. A message was sent to the Foreign Affairs Division, Police Department, Bangkok, Thailand. This was the NCB of Thailand. The message asked for information about Bongsang. Within twelve hours the NCB in Tokyo had passed on to Osaka the return information from Bangkok. Anant Bongsang was well known to the police and was wanted on a charge of contracting prostitution.

A second message was received from Bangkok informing Tokyo that Bongsang had a Japanese contact named Inaba Kondo. Copies of both messages were sent to the General Secretariat in St. Cloud with a request for any information in the Secretariat's files on the two men.

Osaka Police began a stake-out of the Locust Club and Willy's. That night a raid was made on the hotel owned by Kondo. Fifteen girls were arrested and charged with being in the country illegally. Later that same night Inaba Kondo was arrested on charges of violating the Antiprostitution Law and the Employment Security Law. Arrested with him at the Locust Club were the two Japanese, Imai Kunishiro and Sakurai Norio, and the Korean, Pak Yung Wan. The three men were charged with violation of the Antiprostitution Law.

Anant Bongsang was arrested in his hotel the same night. He was charged with conspiring to contract prostitution but, instead of being detained in Osaka, was sent to Interpol-Tokyo to await extradition proceedings from Thailand.

Toshio Harada, otherwise known as Trader Willy, was arrested and charged with conspiring to contract prostitution.

The body of the Thai girl, Patma Vanee, was discovered the following day. She had been shot once through the head. Charges of murder were then placed against Inaba Kondo, Pak Yung Wan, Imai Kunishiro and Sakurai Norio. A charge of accessory to murder was lodged against Shinko Kondo. All these persons are now awaiting trial.

Chapter 3

The man in charge of the Interpol police section that deals with counterfeits, frauds, and forgeries has been with the organization since 1948. A former French police inspector who is fluent in four languages, he has spent more time working at Interpol than anyone except the Secretary General. During these years he's had a ringside seat from which to watch the international game of cops and robbers.

It is his opinion that crime is on the increase at a rate of about 10 percent per year in every category. He had some interesting things to say about today's criminal.

Gone from the scene, for the most part, is the old-style professional hood who spoke from the side of his mouth and wore turned-up collars and a tough scowl. The criminal today is better informed generally about everything he does and can do, as well as about what the police do and can do. He makes use of travel facilities that can whisk him from one continent to another in a matter of hours. He has the services of modern technology to supply him with nearly perfect false identity and other documentation.

To keep up with him, the police need to move with comparable speed and pass out information at an even faster pace. Interpol is doing just that and continually searches for newer and better ways to stay ahead of the criminal.

Counterfeit money, to take one example, can be printed and distributed around the world within days. Last year, authorities seized 30 million counterfeit American dollars. How much more was printed and is in circulation is anybody's guess. The printing is of such high quality that more often than not it takes an expert to spot it as counterfeit.

Money isn't the only thing printed. There's a big market for counterfeit traveler's checks. Easily negotiable, welcomed by those businesses catering to tourists, it has provided another lucrative source of income.

To pass the false money and checks, good identification is needed. This need creates a peripheral business for certain professional printers. False passports or cleverly altered stolen ones, identity cards, driver's licenses, and government documents are manufactured to ease the way of the traveling criminal.

Without question, the king of these nonviolent thieves is the international swindler, or con man. Intelligent, personable, fluent in several languages, and armed with all sorts of documentation to further his schemes, he is the most slippery and exasperating type of adversary for the police.

His imagination is fantastic. His ideas for bilking the public range from international business frauds to sales of nonexistent property or other elaborate hoaxes designed to part people from their money.

Last year, this department of Interpol handled more than 2,200 cases of fraud. Not all of these frauds involved property or securities changing hands across continents. Some of them dealt with more mundane objects. For example, pigs.

•

The people who filled the rented hall on Bay Street in Toronto were almost all newly arrived German immigrants. Many of them spoke only German, while the others had a limited knowledge of English. They had assembled to hear a talk by a most extraordinary man. His name was John Cooper.

He, too, was a recent arrival in Canada. Although he had a British passport, he spoke fluent German and was well known to the leaders of the sizable German community in and around Toronto.

Cooper was one of those fortunate types who seem to have been more gifted than their fellow men. Tall, with the well-conditioned body of an athlete, he appeared to be about forty years old. He had a strong jaw, lively blue eyes, even white teeth, and a warm, sincere smile. His intelligence, while obvious, was not the type that can so often irritate others.

People who met him for the first time invariably came

away convinced they had met a very special person, someone they would like to see again. He had a good sense of humor and endless patience, it was said, in listening to people others considered boring.

His passport showed his true age to be fifty-five, something that never failed to elicit comments about face lifts, health farms, and fitness programs. He bore the remarks with good-natured humility, which only enhanced his image. If anything, he seemed to welcome the banter.

Now, as he walked onto the small stage, smiling and nodding to the audience, he moved toward the microphone and waited to be introduced.

He was there at the special request of one of the German community leaders, Helmut Faber, a man with whom Cooper had spent a great deal of time since coming to Toronto. Faber was a long-time resident of the city and the owner of a department store on King Street.

Faber began to read from a sheet of paper. "John Cooper," he said, "might best be described as a practical philosopher. He is a man with an idea that can change our lives, now, today." This part of the introduction had been supplied by Cooper. Faber had been more than willing to use it as he was not, by his own admission, an adept or imaginative public speaker.

"I first met Mr. Cooper in my store a few months ago. He came to me to discuss his idea which he'll be telling you about tonight. He chose me because I'm well known to most of you. As he speaks perfect German, you'll have no trouble understanding him."

He stepped aside to let Cooper address the group. "I suppose," Cooper said, "I should tell you something about myself." He spoke easily in a rich baritone.

"I came to Canada for much the same reason that you did—basically, to begin a new life. Some of you have come to work here and some to retire here. I know you've found the money you brought with you doesn't go very far."

There were nods of agreement from the audience. It was

true. Canada had turned out to be more expensive than they had thought when they left their homes in Germany.

"Fortune has been good to me," Cooper said. "I'm still young enough to make a new life and a good living." His tone and manner became more intense. "That, the business of making money in a strange land, is what I'm going to talk to you about tonight. I have a personal philosophy about making money—who makes it and who doesn't." He gave the listeners a chance to digest this before continuing.

"Essentially, it's that old adage that those who have it make it and those who don't, don't make it. Well, my background is business and I can truthfully say I've been successful. I made my first million dollars before I was thirty. I learned something while I made that money. Simply stated, it's that you must give back to life what you take from it. Each man has a duty to his fellow man. My plans in Canada are to make it possible for others to benefit from my experience." He paused and looked around the hall as if trying to make eye contact with every person.

"Call it a debt, if you will. Laugh, if you will, but I feel a moral obligation to give back a little of what I've received."

Cooper spent the next half hour explaining why he felt it was very hard for the average person to get rich. After paying out normal living expenses, he said, there's no money left to invest. Money is a tool the rich use as leverage to get more. Almost all investment programs are geared to give such a small return that only large investors can make substantial gains from them.

He had learned, over the years, that the only way for the small man to have a chance was to group together with others. Here again, there was a problem. Even if a large pool was formed by the have-nots, the avenues of investment remained the same. Things like savings accounts, stocks, bonds, or mutual funds still wouldn't pay enough for each person to get ahead. What was needed was something an individual could own and control. As this immediately put the large institutions out of reach, what was left?

29

Well, that was what he had spent so much time discussing with Helmut Faber, who had been so excited by the ideas that he had heard that he had arranged to have them all get together this night.

There was an obvious air of interest when Cooper backed away to let Faber take the microphone. Faber spoke briefly, explaining that those who were interested in learning exactly what Cooper had in mind could remain and be given time for a private interview.

Almost at once, questions were yelled out from the floor, asking for more specific facts. All that had been said, it was pointed out, was that Cooper had a good idea, but it might be nice to be given more information before any private talks.

Cooper came forward, raising his hands to quiet the audience. He hadn't meant to be vague, he said, only the nature of his project could be better explained in private as there would certainly be many time-consuming questions.

He let himself be shouted down. Smiling, evidently very much at ease, he indicated that as it appeared to be the desire of everyone, he would go ahead and explain.

"There is a large piece of land," he said, "located about three miles south of Sunderland, on Highway 12. Some of you may know where that it. The land is mine but is officially owned by a company called Consolidated Livestock Growers of Canada. I'm the president of this firm. Mr. Faber is one of the directors. At the moment, the only things on the land are a few buildings. Whether or not anything else is developed on that land is really up to you and others like you."

"Are you planning a cooperative farm?" someone called out.

"Not exactly. As I said, the name is Consolidated Livestock Growers of Canada. There will be animals on the farm. To be direct, pigs."

This caused a stir. A lot of pigs were raised in the region, but if this man were suggesting investing in a pig farm, he was on the wrong track.

Cooper gave them time to settle down. "Yes," he said. "Pigs, but with a difference." He leaned forward. "My company will sell shares. Each share will represent one pig. The shareholder will also pay for six months' food for his pig. The care and responsibility of the pig will be the burden of the company. At the end of the six months, the shareholder may either sell his pig back to the company at a guaranteed profit of 40 percent or continue to pay for the food until a litter is born to the pig. He will then be able to get 40 percent on the sale of the litter. If by chance the original pig dies, the company guarantees to supply another animal to the shareholder."

Faber now took over the microphone. "Now we will give those of you who want it a chance to speak privately to Mr. Cooper and me. Slips of paper will be passed among you. If you're interested in continuing with this, write your name and address on the paper and stay in your seat. The rest of you, please leave after the slips have been distributed."

There were 140 people in the hall. Only eleven left after the paper had been passed out. Cooper and Faber looked over the collected names, and Faber announced they would begin seeing people immediately in a small office behind the stage.

Helmut Faber was very pleased with the results of the meeting. He was even more happy that he had taken advantage of Cooper's offer to become one of the company directors. He had great faith in the venture and, from the beginning, had enthusiastically backed Cooper and introduced him to the immigrants. In Cooper, he saw a chance to help his people and also, himself. Helmut Faber was not a man with an aversion to making money.

In the little office the exact terms of the program were detailed. The price per share, or per pig, was one hundred dollars. The food for the six months was another seven dollars and fifty cents per month, payable in advance along with the money for the pig.

There was more to the plan than just owning an animal. The program was a participating one. An open house was to be held every Sunday on the property, called Hogville. There were picnic tables, a small playground and trees, and future plans to have a restaurant.

Three more farms, it was explained, were even now being considered for purchase. There was no telling how large the firm could become. It all depended on the number of investors. The investor could buy as many pigs or shares as he could afford. However, Cooper was quick to add, no matter how many pigs any one investor owned, all the investors would receive the same treatment.

On the open-house Sundays, the shareholders would come for the day, to meet each other, to picnic, and to meet their pigs. They were invited to bring along any guests they wished. Sort of like driving to the country to see a country cousin, Cooper kept saying, much to everyone's amusement.

When the night came to an end, Consolidated Livestock Growers of Canada had ninety-four shareholders and the promises of twenty-three other people who hadn't brought cash or their checkbooks with them.

•

The following week, advertisements began to appear in the local newspapers, including the German-language *Courier*. The ads drew well. People who inquired were invited to spend a Sunday at Hogville. Usually, the ones who made the trip to the farm came back as new shareholders.

The size of the investments varied. Many bought only one share but others bought many more. The biggest single investment came from a man from Cleveland. After spending a day at Hogville, he presented the company with a check for sixty thousand dollars for six hundred pigs.

Shortly afterward, the three farms that had been under consideration were bought by the company. However, the main farm, Hogville, was still the center of attraction. As promised by Cooper, a restaurant serving soft drinks, sandwiches, hotdogs, and hamburgers was installed. The company was prospering, and the shareholders were delighted.

The event that attacted the most attention and amusement was the meeting between pig and owner. This was always done with a bit of ceremony. The pig and shareholder were brought face to face in a small shack reserved for this purpose. The pig, scrubbed clean by the hired hands, came into the shack from one door, while Cooper escorted the shareholder in by another door. The pig would have a brightly colored ear tag with the owner's name printed on it.

Later, as the company got bigger and bigger, it took a special request before a shareholder could meet his pig. There was just too much livestock on the land for the pigs to be rounded up, cleaned, and shown to the owners.

The first dividends were paid promptly. The company books showed that some three hundred shareholders received more than eighty thousand dollars. Most of them reinvested their earnings in more pigs. As word of the success of the program spread, the membership swelled.

Many of the original investors now emptied out savings accounts, sold off their securities, and put their money into the company. The firm started talking seriously about buying five more farms and even discussed the possibiity of a franchise operation both in Canada and in the United States.

During this time, Cooper became something of a hero to one special group. It was that group of immigrants with whom he'd started the business. They were outspoken in praise of him and steered everyone they could to his company. They were the best advertisements he could have.

Many people searched Cooper out at Hogville to thank him personally. He was always at the farm on Sundays. Helmut Faber, along with the other two directors of the firm, rarely went to Hogville. He was content to take his profits and check the company books periodically. It was really a one-man show, with Cooper the ringmaster.

Cooper was an easy man to speak to. He was not at all changed by the success of his operation and, if anything, was even more congenial than before. He seemed to go out of his way to meet the shareholders and spend time with them.

Another dividend of close to one hundred thousand dollars was paid to the shareholders. According to Cooper, there were now more than twenty thousand pigs on the four farms. Or as he liked to put it, "a $2-million investment."

An amusement arcade and a swimming pool were added to Hogville. Each Sunday Cooper could be found, dressed in work clothes, surrounded by pigs and shareholders.

Helmut Faber had started with a ten-pig investment. He

now owned 120 animals. As he also participated in the company profits, he was beginning to stack up a tidy piece of change and never lost an opportunity to praise Cooper, whom he called a genius.

Then, on a warm Friday afternoon in April, Farber received a phone call from Cooper at his store. Cooper had decided it was urgent that the firm acquire some new land. There were too many pigs on the four farms and if the company was to continue its expansion, new property was needed. He'd heard of a large parcel of land at a good price, near Ottawa. He thought it best to dash up there before it was snapped up by some else. He wanted Faber to take charge of Hogville the next Sunday as he didn't expect to return in time.

Faber, though always interested in the operation, explained that he didn't know enough about the farm to be of much use. He reminded Cooper that he rarely went to Hogville, didn't know his way around.

Cooper assured him that it would be an easy Sunday. There were no requests to meet pigs, and any other problems could be taken care of by the farm workers.

Reluctantly, Faber agreed. It was a bad weekend for him as he'd half expected to spend Sunday in his store looking over some new stock. However, Cooper was not only a business associate but a good friend. He wished him a good trip and hung up the phone before it occured to him to ask Cooper why he was interested in property some 250 miles away. Finally, Faber decided it didn't matter. Cooper must have a good reason. He put the thought from his mind.

Chapter **4**

Dorval International Airport in Montreal is served by thirty airlines as well as being the home base for both the International Civil Aviation Organization and the International Air Transport Assocation.

That bit of information didn't at all interest the passenger who held a first-class ticket on Swissair Flight 161, leaving for Zürich at nine-forty that evening. He was more concerned about getting on board the DC-10 and settling down for the long trip that would take him to Switzerland.

He'd dined earlier at an excellent French restaurant in downtown Montreal, on roast pork. The waiter had complimented him on his French accent and politely asked if he were indeed French. He told the waiter he wasn't, rather he was German.

While waiting to get on the plane, he struck up a conversation with a German businessman who was taking the same flight. He introduced himself to the businessman as Gerhart Richter from Düsseldorf.

Richter's fellow passenger, named Heinrich Kraft, was delighted to tell Richter that he too, was from Düsseldorf. A round, middle-aged man with a wife and three daughters, Kraft was on a business trip investigating property sites for a Swiss client.

Kraft found Richter to be a pleasant and interesting companion. Later, he was to remember that Richter had said he had been visiting a sister in Montreal and regretted not having more than a few hours to look at the city.

He was also to remember that oddly enough, although he, Kraft, spoke freely about his business, Richter never mentioned what he did for a living. All he got from Richter was the information that Richter was taking a short Swiss holiday before returning to Düsseldorf.

They had a smooth and easy flight. Kraft gave Richter his business card and asked him to get in touch. He found Richter one of the most fascinating conversationalists he had ever met and hoped to see more of him. They parted company in Zürich's Kloten International Airport. Kraft was not to see Richter again.

It was a beautiful Sunday morning in Zürich, surprisingly warm for that time of year.

.

It was also promising to be a beautiful and unseasonably warm morning that same Sunday in Toronto when Helmut Faber got into his car for the drive to Hogville.

He arrived just before nine o'clock. He was pleased, because nine was the hour the shareholders were admitted. He introduced himself to the workers and went to look at the pigs.

His first reaction upon seeing the pigs was that there weren't nearly as many as there should have been. Evidently, Cooper had transferred more than two thirds of them to the other farms. That didn't make sense to Faber as Hogville was the showcase for the firm and also the largest of the farms. This troubled him.

He was more troubled later that morning when he received a phone call asking when the firm planned to pay a long overdue food bill that now totaled seventy thousand dollars. Faber was shocked. It was inconceivable that Cooper would allow such a thing to happen. The man was much too careful about everything to be careless about bills.

He explained to the man that he was a director of the firm and would personally see to it that a check for the full amount was sent off first thing the next morning, Monday. He made up his mind to speak to Cooper and ask him to be more attentive to such things.

The idea of a bill that size made Faber uneasy. Later, he was sorry he had assured the man it would be paid the next day. Cooper might not be back from his trip, and the only other person authorized to write checks that large was the company attorney. He decided he'd better contact the lawyer. There was no financial problem, Faber knew. The last time he had checked the books, they showed Consolidated Livestock Growers to have $2 million on deposit. Of course, a large percentage of that was reserve to pay dividends, but that still left more than enough to pay any bills.

By the time the day ended, Faber was more than a little irritated with Cooper. Obviously the man was running a one-man show. No one knew anything about anything. He had asked the workers why the pigs had been transferred, but they didn't know. He had tried to find out how many pigs were on the premises but was told that only Cooper knew the figure. When he asked how many pigs were on each of the other farms, he was again told that he would have to speak with Cooper. He drove back to Toronto that night in a foul mood.

Monday morning brought more warm weather—and disaster. The attorney discovered the firm's bank account couldn't cover a check for one thousand dollars, much less seventy thousand.

Faber, with the attorney, at once tried to contact Cooper, but he hadn't returned. They waited one more day, then, with deepening suspicions, contacted the other two directors of the firm. A decision was reached.

A firm of chartered accountants was called in with instructions to investigate every detail. The first thing done was to count all the pigs. There were only two thousand on the four farms instead of the twenty thousand that represented the investors' shares.

On March 2, the story broke in the newspapers. Hogville had gone broke. A receivership was set up as the firm was declared bankrupt. An effort was made to salvage what was left of the shareholder's pigs and money.

As for John Cooper? Well . . .

•

In Zürich, Gerhart Richter bought a copy of a Toronto newspaper and read about the collapse of Consolidated Livestock Growers of Canada. It was not a problem for him.

His Zürich bank account was handsomely enriched by the $1.8 million he had transferred from Canada.

All that had been John Cooper—the passport, driver's license, and other identification—had been torn up and flushed down a toilet in Montreal.

Richter's business in Zürich was to close out his bank account by another transfer of funds, this time to a bank in Luxembourg. He had made the necessary arrangements and had lingered on because he felt he owed himself time to relax and do absolutely nothing.

He was moving his money from Switzerland to cut any links between Canada and Zürich. He knew that soon the police would be investigating, and he was making sure they would have little to go on. As it was, it was going to be nearly impossible for them, he thought. They would be looking for a British citizen named John Cooper, not a German national named Gerhart Richter.

He decided that after his trip to Luxembourg he would spend a few weeks in Paris. He knew Paris well and spring was certainly the best time of year to enjoy that city. He wasn't sure how long he would stay, but after Paris he had very definite plans. He would go to Spain—Barcelona, to be exact. It was his favorite city. There he would rent a large villa overlooking the Mediterranean and begin the life he had always dreamed about: the life of a rich playboy.

He had come a long way in just four years. Four years earlier he had left a cell in Fresnes, the prison on the outskirts of Paris. He had been serving a two-year sentence for fraud. The irony of it was that he had made almost nothing out of it. From Richter's point of view it had been the low point of his life. But now things were quite different.

After his release from Fresnes, he had gone to Central America. His luck picked up there, and he made a little money. From there it had been Venezuela, where a quick little scheme had given him the stake to set up his Canadian venture.

Yes, he decided, Spain would be ideal. It was warmer in the south of Europe and, of course, he did speak perfect

Spanish. He himself thought that his ability to speak different languages so fluently was his strongest talent.

The more he thought about Barcelona while relaxing in Zürich, the more anxious he became to get there. Finally he decided to cancel the trip to Paris and go directly to Spain after Luxembourg.

•

Meanwhile, in Toronto, it had become time to call in the police. The first item of importance was to locate John Cooper. This, naturally, proved impossible. Quickly, certain the search must be widened, the national police force, the Royal Canadian Mounted Police, was contacted, and a nationwide hunt for Cooper got underway.

Countless leads were run down. Almost everyone known to have associated with Cooper was questioned. Helmut Faber, angry and chagrined, offered a five-thousand-dollar reward for information leading to the arrest and conviction of Cooper.

It was decided that Cooper had fled the country. In Ottawa, the Royal Canadian Mounted Police serve as the National Central Bureau for Interpol. At once they sent a dispatch letter to Scotland Yard. A copy of the letter was routinely sent to Interpol's General Secretariat in St. Cloud.

Included in the dispatch letter was Cooper's British passport number, taken from Canadian immigration records. Also included were all the available facts about Cooper and the crime he was wanted for.

In two days, Scotland Yard informed Ottawa that neither the British Home Officer or Immigration had any record of a passport issued to the man named in the dispatch letter. If he was traveling on a British passport, it was a forged one.

The National Central Bureau in Ottawa asked the General Secretariat for help. From St. Cloud, Interpol went into action. The hunt was now worldwide.

A circular was sent to all the member nations. This circular contained all the information Interpol had on Cooper. Every National Central Bureau checked its own records and the country's police files to see if they had any information on the wanted man.

Two weeks passed. Nothing came back into the General Secretariat to indicate that they were getting closer to capturing John Cooper.

•

Gerhart Richter arrived in Barcelona and checked into the Hotel Diplomatic. All his important business had been completed successfully. He planned to stay at the hotel until he could find just the house he wanted. He contacted several rental agents and made appointments to see them. He was in no hurry.

•

At the National Central Bureau in France, a police officer turned up a piece of information that caused a ripple of interest. Some years ago, he had arrested a man who fitted the description of John Cooper. It had been a fraud case and the man had been sentenced to a two-year prison term in Fresnes. The only problem was that the man had been a Frenchman, named Henri Balin.

The lead was followed up. A set of fingerprints and a photo of Balin were sent by the General Secretariat on its phototelegraphic equipment to the National Central Bureau in Ottawa.

Helmut Faber without hesitation identified the picture of Balin as that of John Cooper. Others made the same unhesitating identification. Ottawa was satisfied. A warrant was issued for Balin's arrest and the information sent to St. Cloud.

A red notice was now issued. It supplied fingerprints, a photo, and an order for immediate arrest. This red notice was circulated to all the member nations of Interpol.

•

Gerhart Richter had paid a year's rent on a two-story house that overlooked the sea. There was a wall around the house with a large enough entrance to permit Richter to drive his new yellow Maserati inside and park it in front of the doorway.

He was happy he had come to Spain. He felt very much at home there. The perfection of his Spanish drew compliments.

People were always surprised to discover he was German.

·

In Wiesbaden, West Germany, the Bundeskriminalamt, National Central Bureau for that nation, made an interesting find. The photograph in the red notice from the General Secretariat matched a photo they had, as did the fingerprints. Their prints and picture identified Balin as a German, named Karl Kraft. He had been held but later released on a fraud charge. His place of birth was Düsseldorf.

·

Gerhart Richter's yellow Maserati, with Richter and an American tourist, Cindy Mathews, showed up in Valencia. They were seen and remembered in many of the night clubs and restaurants. They had created quite a stir before heading back to Barcelona after five hectic days and nights.

·

In Düsseldorf, the search for Karl Kraft led to the house of another Kraft, Heinrich Kraft. After being shown a photograph of Karl Kraft, he said he thought it was the same man he'd flown to Zürich with from Montreal. He gave the police a new name, Gerhart Richter.

In Bern, the capital of Switzerland, the Bureau Central Swiss is the National Central Bureau of Interpol. The name Gerhart Richter was sent there to be checked out. Swiss immigration records confirmed that the wanted man had entered the country at Kloten International Airport. His hotel was located, as was his date of departure for Luxembourg.

The National Central Bureau in Luxembourg, at the Palais de Justice, made some investigations and quickly turned up the information that Richter had stayed there six days and then left by plane for Paris, where he was to make a connection on Air France Flight 493, leaving daily at 12:25 P.M. for Barcelona, Spain.

Now the General Secretariat sent out a new red notice. This one listed all of the names used by the hunted man as well as his fingerprints and photograph.

•

Richter suggested to Cindy Mathews that it might be nice if she were to stay through the summer with him. Her plans had been to follow the coastline, along the French and Italian Rivieras, and then perhaps, if she had enough time, to continue to Greece before going back to the United States. She liked Richter. He was handsome and a lot of fun and didn't mind spending a lot of money for a good time. She decided to stay.

•

In Madrid, the Comisaria General de Investigacion Criminal, Interpol-Spain, worked quickly. Spanish immigration established that a Gerhart Richter had entered the country at Barcelona International Airport on Air France Flight 493.

An intense investigation was begun, centering on that port city. Rapidly, the information came into police headquarters. Guest records at the Hotel Diplomatic showed that Richter had spent eight days there. Then, the same day, the rental agency that handled the transaction on Richter's house was located.

Two plainclothes detectives parked their car in front of Richter's house. It was early evening, and they found no one at home. They sat down to wait, watching the entrance to the house from the car.

•

The yellow Maserati came screeching to a halt, almost hitting the police car. Gerhart Richter, dressed in slacks and a pullover sweater, got out and ran around the car to open the door for Cindy Mathews. As he bent down to the low door of the Maserati, he saw a look of surprise on her face. She was staring at something over his lowered shoulders. At the same time he realized that someone or something was right behind him. He spun around.

Two men were flanking him. One of them extended a hand to show a police badge.

"Police," the man said. "Are you Gerhart Richter?"

"No," Richter replied. He spoke in Spanish but his accent

was definitely French. "My name is Henri Balin. You've made a mistake."

The detective nodded. "We are also looking for a Henri Balin."

"In that case, I suppose you want me to go with you." This time the Spanish was impeccable. He turned to Cindy Mathews and casually waved goodbye.

The two detectives led him to the police car. He knew he was destined to sit in a Spanish jail until the extradition proceedings were completed and the long trip to Canada begun.

It was unfortunate that he had had only two months in which to enjoy his playboy life. He said so to the two detectives.

Chapter 5

In apprehending Henri Balin, alias John Cooper, Interpol again demonstrated its capability to coordinate a swift hunt for a wanted man. Despite his experience, intelligence, and linguistic abilities, Balin could not escape the web of information that pinpointed him for the authorities. His carefully prepared plans for his numerous identities were not enough to ensure his freedom.

Anyone less prepared, it would seem, should be caught more rapidly. Therefore, when a search was launched for a young American couple whose only language was English and who used their own passports, it was assumed they would be found in a few days. It didn't work out quite that way.

•

Jerry Young and his wife Doris landed at Malpensa International Airport in Milan on July 1, 1973. Both were very excited, as they had been looking forward to this day for a full year. They'd spent countless evenings in New York talking about it. Ahead of them now were four glorious weeks to explore the art of Italy.

Jerry was a frustrated artist. He had been trying to sell his paintings for six years without one sale to his name. It had made him a bitter young man. He had begun to doubt his talent.

Doris had no such doubts. She was convinced that one day his work would be famous and exhibited in the major art museums of the world.

She felt this strongly enough to have insisted that Jerry devote his time to painting in their New York apartment while she supported them. Her parents and her friends thought she was crazy to live like that. She may have been the only person in the city who believed his work had any merit. At any rate, her job as a registered nurse enabled them to live and even put away the money for the trip to Italy.

The trip had been Doris's idea. She thought if Jerry had a chance to see the work of the old masters in their Italian setting, it might give him the boost he so desperately needed to get his career going.

She was a short, thin girl with intense brown eyes. Although she was seven years younger than her husband, she impressed people as the more mature of the two. This maturity, however, did not apply in her feelings for Jerry. She adored him and would do anything for him.

Jerry, at thirty-one, was not unaware of his wife's devotion. He was a stocky, muscular man with a beard and long dark hair worn loosely over his shoulders. Before deciding to become an artist on a full-time basis, he had held a variety of low-paying jobs in factories and gas stations. His face might have been called handsome except for its constant sullen expression. In the five years of his marriage to Doris he had never brought home any income.

Just before boarding the plane in New York, she had once more explained to her parents why she wanted the trip for Jerry. They listened with the same silent contempt in their eyes they always showed when she mentioned his name. They felt Jerry's sole talent was living off their daughter's earnings.

Jerry, always enthusiastic about the trip, had become even more so as the time got closer. For him, it was also a chance to get away from the people who wondered why he never worked or, worse still, to his thinking, why he couldn't sell any of his paintings. He was sick and tired, he had said many times to Doris, of having to explain his way of life.

Their plans were to stay only one day in Milan. Jerry wanted to see Leonardo da Vinci's *Last Supper*. After Milan, it was to be Florence. They had agreed that Jerry would pick the places to go while Doris's job would be to take care of the finances. They had exactly five hundred dollars in traveler's checks and their return tickets home on the twenty-two-to-forty-five-day excursion plan.

The expected one day in Milan turned into five days. Jerry

had discovered and become fascinated with the scientific models of da Vinci that were displayed in the Museum of Science and Technology. When Doris reminded him that they still had a lot of places to visit, he reminded her that he was the one to choose the towns to see. As usual, she gave in to his wishes.

When they did take the train to Florence and got their first look at the city, they were overwhelmed. They had originally allowed one week to see Florence but now realized they needed more time. Jerry decided they would remain until they had seen everything, even if it meant seeing nothing else.

One evening, shortly after their arrival, they were having coffee at an outside table in front of the Il Roga restaurant, which had a reputation for being inexpensive and catering to tourists who knew their way around. Here they met another American couple about their own age. Soon they became friends, and each evening the four of them would meet for a sharing of conversation and a liter of red wine.

Jerry and Doris learned that the other couple had been in Europe for more than two years, supporting themselves by taking odd jobs that weren't too strict about work permits. Jerry began to talk to Doris about doing the same thing.

Doris objected. It wasn't practical. There was always the chance they wouldn't find any work and would run out of money. Jerry didn't argue with her, but he was making his plans. Meanwhile, the time in Florence was moving out from under them as quickly as their money.

The last night before they had to go back to Milan to catch their return flight to New York, Jerry announced that he had found a job. He would be working as a bartender in Palermo. It wasn't much, he explained, but it would let them continue to stay in Europe and later on, after the summer season, they could find something else. All they had to do, he said, was to get to Palermo. The job had been promised by the owner of the bar, an Italian-American who spoke English perfectly. He would tend bar nights and during the days work on his painting. It was the perfect setup.

46

They argued about it all night. Doris kept talking about being practical, Jerry about his career. He finally convinced her by pointing out that she could always get a job if they had to return to New York. Why not try it? What did they really have to lose except her old job? And besides, she was really enjoying Italy as much as he, wasn't she? They left for Palermo with high hopes and thirty dollars.

They checked into the Hotel Sausele, near the train station. Their double room cost seven dollars a day. While Doris unpacked, Jerry went to see the bar where he would be working.

He returned with the news that there was no job. The man in Florence who had claimed to be the owner of the bar had lied. He had been employed in the bar himself as a waiter. The actual owner had sympathized with Jerry, but needed no help.

Doris was furious and, for the first time in their marriage, told him that he was worthless and might well end up a bum. After the inevitable fight her words caused, Jerry ran from the room in a rage. He came back two hours later.

In reply to her question as to where he had gone, he flung a fistful of Italian banknotes on the bed. "There," he said. "Now shut your mouth."

"Where did you get the money?"

He explained he had cashed a personal check for two hundred dollars' worth of lire.

"But we don't have two hundred dollars in our bank account," she told him.

"Who cares?" he replied. "It'll take them a month to find that out." He showed her a pocket calendar. It was August 1, 1973.

They remained in Palermo another week, spending most of the time fighting with each other. Jerry kept saying they should go to England. Doris kept saying they should get back to the States and see that there was money in the account to cover the check. Jerry told her it was too late and that anyway, nothing would happen.

Finally, she capitulated. As far as she was concerned, she

told him, he could run things the way he wanted. She would just tag along. Later, she was to say she went along with him because she was afraid he would walk out on her.

They had enough money left to travel to England, entering the country at Folkestone on the boat train from France.

In London, they immediately increased their cash reserves by passing a bad check for one hundred dollars. This time, Doris offered no objections. She had committed herself to whatever Jerry wanted to do. Ten minutes after cashing the check they spotted a Fiat sedan with the keys in the ignition. They took the car and drove to Reading, left the car in a parking lot in front of the railroad station, and found a hotel for the night.

In the morning they cashed another check, for fifty dollars, and then rented a car. They headed for Cornwall. The car was rented for two days, and Doris was beginning to enjoy what was going on. It was the first time that she could remember ever feeling so free of responsibility. As for Jerry, he was having the time of his life. He told Doris that if they were careful, they could live this way indefinitely.

On August 12 in a sporting-goods store in Exeter they purchased a tennis racket which they paid for with a hundred-dollar check, taking the change in pounds.

On August 16, they abandoned the rented car in London and took the night train for Paris with a morning connection to Nice. They joked about spending part of the summer on the French Riviera.

After checking into the Hôtel des Nations in Nice, they immediately cashed a check for seventy-five dollars. Doris cashed this one and couldn't get over how easily she managed to do it. Any earlier qualms she may have had were completely gone by this time.

On August 20 they cashed their largest check to date: three hundred dollars, in the Palais de la Méditerranée, a popular Nice gambling casino.

It had turned into a game for both Jerry and Doris. Their only problem now was where to go next. Fortunately or unfortunately, depending on the viewpoint, they had two books of checks in their luggage.

Ten more days was all they dared to stay in Nice. They decided to go to Germany next. They arrived in Aachen by train on August 31.

They found accommodations in the Hotel Frankfurter Hof at 30-32 Bahnhofstrasse. The first day was spent touring the city. Doris especially enjoyed the town hall, where the treasures of the cathedral and Charlemagne were displayed. Also, that first day, they met an Australian, John Dunlop. The three of them spent a lot of time together, although at no time did they tell Dunlop what they were doing.

Dunlop kept talking about Hamburg and what a fun city it was. If he weren't running low on funds, he told the Youngs, he would love to go back there for at least another week.

On September 7, Doris rented a car, and the three of them threw their luggage into the trunk. They were off to Hamburg, with Dunlop coming along as their guest. By now he believed Jerry to be a successful New York artist. There was one quick stop made, just before leaving Aachen. This was a restaurant, where they ate lunch and where Jerry cashed a fifty-dollar check.

Dunlop steered them to a hotel close to the Reeperbahn, the night-life section. The hotel was the Paulinenhof, and the three of them shared the same room. Dunlop stayed with them for one week and left. The Youngs, liking what they saw of Hamburg, decided to spend a longer time there. They stayed about a month. The car they had rented was found on October 3 in the three-story garage of the luxury-class Atlantic Hotel.

On October 17, in Heidelberg, the police were told that an American couple had tried to cash a personal check in the Hotel Goldener Falke, in the old city near the University. The couple had shown two different identifications. One was a passport, the other a French credit card. The names had not been the same. When asked about this, the man and woman had run from the hotel. The name on the passport, an American passport, had been Doris Young.

At the same time that the Heidelberg Police were receiving this information, Jerry and Doris were renting a car. Frightened, they had decided it was time to leave Germany and cross over to France and then to Switzerland. It was the first time they had fumbled while trying to cash a check. They made a promise to be more careful in the future.

Heading toward Switzerland, they stopped in Besançon, where they passed a seventy-five-dollar check and also left the rented car.

Then it was on to Lausanne, Switzerland. Here they agreed to rest awhile and let things cool off. With that in mind, they took a double room in the Hotel Transit, near the railroad station. On Christmas Eve, they had dinner at the fancy Lausanne Palace Hotel and cashed a two-hundred-dollar check to celebrate the occasion.

The first of the year found them in Naples, restless, tired of the regulated neatness of Switzerland. After two weeks, they left an unpaid bill at the Hotel Rex and rented a car. They were down to their last check and thought France offered better prospects than Italy.

In Lyon, they opened a bank account and received two checkbooks with fifty checks in each. They passed all of these, making a sweep through France, Belgium, and Switzerland. The last check was cashed in Geneva on February 15. In all, the two checkbooks added $6,000 to their money.

During all this time, Doris and Jerry felt as if what they were doing weren't real. "Sort of being in a dream," Doris said later. "I always had the idea that we weren't doing anything wrong and that one day we'd wake up in our beds in our New York apartment."

After a little debate, Austria was chosen as the next place to go. Doris had wanted to go up to the Scandinavian countries, but Jerry preferred Austria. As usual, he got his way. The afternoon of March 2, Doris and Jerry checked into the Hotel Austria in the center of Vienna.

Because it was their first trip into that country, they were sure it was a safe place for them. Like any other tourists they saw the sights. They were especially impressed by the view of Vienna from the north tower of St. Stephen's Cathedral. They made four trips to it while in the city. Nights found them regular customers at the Griechenbeisl, a beer parlor dating back to the fifteenth century. It was a popular place to drink beer and listen to accordion and zither music.

Finally, Jerry decided it was time to move on. Before leaving, they opened another bank account and received a total of 150 blank checks. They began cashing them on March 24. A new method let them pass them faster than ever. They would split up and each would cash six checks. Most of the time, they would make a small purchase and pay for the merchandise with a check larger than the amount of the goods.

Traveling by rented car, they stopped off to cash checks in Salzbourg (April 1), Dornbrin (April 6), Villach (April 10), and finally St. Poelten (April 15). The car they'd been using was found on a street in Luxembourg on the second of May.

During a ten-day check-cashing binge in Brussels that ended on the eleventh of May, they picked up the equivalent of $3,400 in francs.

Doris mentioned to Jerry that she had liked Germany, so they made a quick trip there, with stops of varying lengths in Rheydt, Herford, and Munich. Another $1,300 was collected.

Jerry now announced that he was ready to visit Scandinavia. On July 1, they had a special dinner to celebrate one year in Europe. The dinner was eaten in the Tudor-style Grill Room of the Hotel Bristol in Oslo, Norway. The hotel had served as Allied Headquarters during the liberation in 1945.

"Let's keep Oslo pure," Jerry said over dinner. "We'll come back here next year again, to the same table, in 1975."

"Good idea," Doris agreed. "We'll make the hotel our headquarters too."

"Yeah," Jerry said. "Maybe one day we'll have a plaque put up for us as well."

Before Doris and Jerry left the table that night, they had decided that a trip to Greece and Turkey might be interesting.

First, however, they planned a trip to England, where they would open another bank account and supply themselves with more blank checks.

"When do you think we'll go home to New York?" Doris asked.

"After Turkey," Jerry told her.

"What if they're looking for us in the States?"

"Then we won't go back," Jerry said. "We can always go live in someplace like Morocco."

They toasted each other late into the night.

Chapter 6

Luigi Cortorillo was agitated. He kept running his hands through his hair while he explained to the police lieutenant how he had been swindled by an American tourist. He shook his fist at the check lying on the police officer's desk.

The lieutenant, trying to quiet Cortorillo, suggested for the fourth time that perhaps a mistake had been made. It was unlikely, in his opinion, that a bad check would have been passed with the person's passport number written on the back of it. It would be better, he thought, to send the check back to the bank in New York for collection.

Cortorillo disagreed. The check had come back marked "insufficient funds." What made the lieutenant think it wouldn't happen again?

Once more the lieutenant explained that he thought Cortorillo was too excited and should resubmit the check. It was surely an honest mistake.

Cortorillo persisted. He wanted some action taken. He had paid out two hundred dollars' worth of lire for that check. It was a lot of money to lose.

The lieutenant jotted down the passport number on a form. He also called the hotel that had been listed on the back of the check as the local address of the tourist.

The Hotel Sausele confirmed the fact that two Americans, Jerry Young and his wife, had been guests. They had left the hotel more than three weeks ago. There was no forwarding address.

The lieutenant handed the check back to Cortorillo and told him to send it back to the New York bank. "It'll be all right," he said. "You'll see."

•

In London, three days later, a Metropolitan Police inspector, after examining a hundred-dollar check that had been returned stamped "insufficient funds," had a search made in the department's records to see if there were any other complaints involving the writer of the check. When he received the answer that there were no complaints, he also suggested that the check be sent back through to the New York bank for collection. He did, however, make an entry on a police form, indicating the name, the passport number, and the date and amount of the check.

He had just about dismissed the incident when he received a phone call from a substation. They'd gotten wind of his request for an inquiry earlier in the day and had come up with the name he had been looking for. An American, Jerry Young, had rented a car in Reading on August 11 and had abandoned it in London. A large sum of money was due. Could there be any connection with the Young the inspector had asked about?

Later that same day a complaint about a check came into Scotland Yard from Exeter. Again, it was a check issued by Jerry Young.

Scotland Yard now took charge of all the information and put out an order to pick up the Youngs. At this point, they were fairly certain they were dealing with professional thieves. The search for the Youngs had begun. The date was September 14, 1973.

.

Three days after the arrest warrant was authorized in London, the French Police became interested in Doris and Jerry. Bad checks had been passed in Nice, so the hunt for the Youngs began there.

Meanwhile, Scotland Yard, the Interpol National Central Bureau for England, contacted the National Central Bureau in France. Their feeling was that Jerry and Doris might have gone to France. Or even if they hadn't, they might have come from there, in which case the French might have some information that could help.

Now that Interpol was involved in the case, the General Secretariat sent out a circular to all the European countries. They hadn't much information, but they could give the passport number and the general physical description of the couple. They also contacted the National Central Bureau in the United States, the Treasury Department, and asked if it were possible to have photographs of the Youngs as well as any other information the Americans could dig up. It was now September 22.

Duplicates of the Youngs' passport photos were received at the General Secretariat on September 25. Something else was received as well on that day: reports from Germany, bad checks from Aachen, and a complaint about a missing rental car. The dossier on the Youngs was getting bulky.

Interpol's machinery moved into high gear. A red notice was sent to all member nations, inside and outside of Europe. As is normal with this type of notice, exact information was given about what type of arrest warrants had been issued as well as photographs of the couple, along with all other facts Interpol had to help identify them. The Youngs were now open to arrest in 120 countries. Interpol had not wasted time. The notices went out on October 5.

The first good chance to catch Jerry and Doris came twelve days later in Heidelberg. The police in that city, responding to a call about two Americans trying to cash a check in the Goldener Falke Hotel while using two identities, sent a man to investigate. As no money had been lost, the police officer didn't show up until the following morning. When he returned to the police station with the name supplied by the hotel, he realized who the couple had been. It was too late, however, to do anything about it except to send the information to the National Central Bureau in Wiesbaden.

In France, with their luck holding, Jerry and Doris passed through the city of Besançon at the very time that a meeting concerning them was being held in the Commissariat Central (main police station). Later, when the police realized a bad check had been cashed by the objects of their discussion on the same day, they would be furious. Actually, the meeting was a routine one. They didn't really expect the Youngs to pass through their city.

In the General Secretariat the dossier got larger. New

reports were coming in from all over. November came and went. The dossier got still bigger. It was hard to fathom. Information about the Youngs was at every border in Europe. It was thought that they had stopped somewhere and gone into hiding. It had become a case of waiting for them to emerge. The first frontier they attempted to cross, it would all be over, or so the general feeling ran.

In Lausanne, Switzerland, the information from the red notice had arrived as a telegram and that piece of paper now lay buried under a stack of other circulars, waiting to be filed. It was getting close to Christmas, and a jolly mood prevailed in the city.

Every evening, at about seven o'clock, the young policeman whose beat included the railroad station would wave hello to the tourist couple staying at the Hotel Transit. Although the couple never spoke to the policeman, nor he to them, they always greeted each other.

Afterward, the Youngs were to say they remembered him very well. "He had such rosy cheeks," Doris said.

Miraculously, their names hadn't shown up when the telegram about the red notice had first arrived in Lausanne. Whoever had checked the hotel registers had done the Youngs a big favor by not spotting them. It was a sample of the luck they enjoyed throughout their travels.

When they did make the move the police had been waiting for, crossing the border into Italy, it was the police who were surprised, not the Youngs.

There had been no magic about it. Traveling by train in a packed second-class compartment, they'd simply gotten passed over in the crowd. The immigration and customs men going through the train had so much to do that they were happy to be able to glance at the two American passports and let things go at that. They hadn't wanted to delay the train, which was behind schedule already.

On January 22, 1974, the Youngs had their closest call. They weren't aware of it. It happened in Lyon, as they were leaving the bank where they had opened an account to get more blank checks.

Michel Girard, a French immigration officer who worked the port in Cherbourg, was in Lyon to visit his sister. As Doris and Jerry stepped through the doors of the bank on their way out, Girard passed them on his way in.

He looked at the couple and started to smile and speak. He knew their faces well even if he couldn't remember their names. He heard them speak to each other in English and cut off his greeting. He must have made a mistake and yet they looked so familiar.

While he wrote a check inside the bank, standing at the counter, he suddenly realized why he knew them. For the past week in Cherbourg, he had been looking at their photographs. Leaving his pen and checkbook behind, he dashed into the street. When he couldn't see them he ran back inside the bank, hoping to find some trace of the Youngs. He was delighted to find out they had opened an account, confirming that it was indeed the wanted couple he'd seen.

A citywide dragnet was immediately put into action by the Lyon Police. Only one hour had elapsed from the time of Girard's positive identification of the Youngs and the alert. That was roughly a half hour too late. The couple was gone, heading for Belgium, via Paris, by train.

The police continued their intensive search for thirty-six hours before deciding that somehow, their quarry had slipped away. After calling off the hunt, they notified Interpol. It proved to be an expensive delay. By March 1, almost all of the six thousand dollars in bad checks had come back through the Lyon bank.

Copies of these checks were coming into the General Secretariat practically on a daily basis. Dispatch letters were sent to the National Central Bureaus asking for more vigorous action in tracking down the Youngs.

While the police redoubled their efforts, Doris and Jerry were sightseeing in Vienna. Their luck had spirited them across more borders with no problems. They were completely unaware that an international hunt was in effect solely for their benefit. At each country's frontier, they filled out the immigration card without a thought of being trapped.

And then, quite unexpectedly, word reached Interpol that the couple had been arrested. Officials waited to hear more news. The arrest had taken place in Brussels. It was April 10, just about six months from the time the police had begun to look for the Youngs.

The eagerly awaited details came through. It had been a mistake. The couple arrested had the same last names and more or less fitted the general descriptions of the Youngs. A fingerprint check had proved them to be a U.S. Army captain and his wife. More infuriating perhaps than this news was the arrival three days later of a new group of checks from an Austrian bank, bearing the Young signatures. As an added attraction, there was even a check cashed in Brussels on the same day the wrong Youngs were arrested.

The couple were living a charmed life. Time went by. The record of their travels was neatly cataloged and filed in the police stations and in the Interpol General Secretariat. Because they were moving around in an indefinite pattern, it was impossible to anticipate them.

On July 17, 1974 the Youngs entered England for the second time at Folkestone. Once more they passed the desks where they had to hand in the immigration cards. Once more the girl behind the desk took their cards and mechanically asked how long they intended to stay in England while stamping a six-month visa into their passports.

They rented a car in London and drove out of the city toward Cornwall, where they had decided to have a little holiday. Along the way, they went past some of the towns they had visited on the first trip.

Doris was to say that it was while driving through this area that she suddenly began to feel uneasy. "Maybe it was a sixth sense or something. I got this thing in my head about us getting caught. I just knew it was going to happen. I kept after Jerry to change his mind about going to Cornwall, but he wouldn't listen."

In the small town of Newton Abbot, Jerry drove through a red light and was stopped by a police car. There were two officers in the car, and while one remained behind the wheel, the other walked over to Jerry and Doris.

After the initial exchange of words, the officer, Jacob Finch, realized he'd probably stopped two American tourists. He was prepared to be lenient.

"I was going to give them a warning, that's all," he said. "Often, visiting drivers aren't used to the positioning of our traffic signals."

The driver's license Jerry Young showed Finch had expired three months before. He hoped the unfamiliar license would pass the officer's inspection. It didn't.

Calmly and politely Finch asked how Jerry had rented the car with the expired license. Doris replied just as politely that she had rented the car, as her license was valid. She offered it to Finch.

Jerry, at this point, explained that Doris wasn't feeling well, and he was driving the car only until they could find a hotel. He continued by saying that he would be more careful about watching for red lights in the future.

Finch didn't reply to this. He was trying to make up his mind about letting them go; was ready, in fact, to suggest a nearby hotel.

Unwisely Jerry filled in the momentary silence with a poor suggestion. "Will you take fifty dollars, Officer, and forget about this?"

At once, Finch ordered the couple to get out of the car. At the same time he signaled his partner to join him. His first reaction to the bribe had been to suspect the couple were carrying narcotics. He meant to search the car.

Jerry made things worse. Instead of getting out of the car, he upped his offer to a hundred dollars. This firmly convinced Finch that something peculiar was going on. He now insisted on Jerry and Doris getting out of the car, locking it, and coming with him and his partner in the police car to the police station.

Doris started crying. Jerry told her to shut up, and Finch had to restrain him from slapping her. They rode in the back of the police car with Doris continuing to cry.

By the time they had reached the police station, Doris had, between sobs, blurted out enough truths to make Finch put in an immediate call to the Metropolitan Police in London.

Within minutes after the call, the Fraud Division of Scotland Yard was notified. The Youngs were to be held until an investigating officer would arrive in Newton Abbot.

Two days later the Youngs were taken to London to be charged and tried. While awaiting a court date, information on their arrest had triggered an unpleasant surprise for them. Not only would they stand before a British court, but each nation that had issued a warrant for them wanted to put them on trial as well.

The four-year prison sentence handed out to them in England may have been just the first of several sentences to follow. As of now, four countries still have holds on the Youngs. The only question is which country will be the next to extradite them when they finish their prison terms.

Chapter 7

While the Youngs may have given the police a long and not so merry chase with their helter-skelter bouncing all over Europe, at least they confined their activities to one continent. And for almost all of this time, their identities and nationalities were known.

A tougher type of police problem arises when a crime is not confined by continental boundaries and when there are not any known names or nationalities. If the stakes in terms of money are high and threaten to grow higher each passing day, rapid action becomes more important. It turns into an international game of hide-and-seek with the prize sometimes being millions of dollars. This is the situation that Interpol finds itself in more often than not.

•

On the night of January 22, 1975, Richard Venner, an American businessman in Paris, invited four other Americans to join him for dinner. For the occasion he chose the Pompadour Restaurant in the Hôtel Meurice on the Rue de Rivoli. The restaurant, patterned after a Bavarian chateau, is both elaborate and expensive.

The cost of a dinner for five presented no problems to Venner. He was, along with his guests, enjoying an all-expenses-paid two-week holiday in Paris. This was their last night in the city, and Venner had promised them an evening to remember.

All of the men, including Venner, worked for a large industrial chemical firm, headquartered in Dallas, Texas. Venner was a company vice-president in charge of marketing. The four men were the four leading salesmen of their respective regions in the United States. The two-week trip was a company-sponsored award for the previous year's sales efforts.

Venner, heavy-set, bluff, and hearty, joked his way through the sumptuous meal. He warned the others to go easy on the wine as there would be a long night ahead of them.

After dinner they took a taxi to Montmartre to explore the night clubs in that district. Shortly after midnight, Venner insisted that they all get in another taxi and go to a different place. There were some objections as everybody was having a good time, but Venner again told them that he had special plans for this night.

He gave the taxi driver an address in Montparnasse. It took about fifteen minutes for the drive. When the taxi pulled up in front of a small bar on a side street there were more objections. However, Venner led the way into the bar and told the others to wait near the door. They did as he said and waited while he went to the back of the bar and had a short conversation with a small, smartly dressed man.

The man Venner had come to see was a Frenchman, Armand Boucher. After the conversation ended, the Americans and Boucher left the bar and squeezed into the Frenchman's car, a two-year-old Renault. He drove them to an apartment house on Avenue de Villiers in the 17th Arrondissement.

They took an elevator to the fifth floor of the building where Boucher ushered them into a large apartment. There, in the lavishly furnished living room, he introduced them to five young and beautiful girls. These girls worked for Boucher, who was known to the Paris Police as an enterprising pimp, with a stable that at times had fifteen girls.

As the couples began to pair off and drinks were passed around, Venner and Boucher completed the financial part of the arrangement.

"I don't have many francs left," Venner said. "How about taking it in American dollars?"

When Boucher agreed, Venner brought out his wallet and handed the Frenchman five one-hundred-dollar bills. Boucher pocketed the money with scarcely a glance at it and then apologized because he had to leave without having even one drink with them. He explained he still had some business to take care of before morning.

He had not lied. He was in a hurry. He had to meet two of his girls who were working in the Bois de Boulogne and collect their money. These two were not among his high-class prostitutes. They worked the passing cars, standing at the edge of the road on the grass and waving to the drivers.

For some time now, Boucher had been thinking about letting them go. Too often to suit him, they were picked up by the police, and then he would have to spend a great deal of time and money to get them out of jail. He much preferred the apartment operation. The girls made more money for him and were less likely to be jailed.

Boucher drove into the Bois de Boulogne, noticing other prostitutes along the tree-lined roads. He had a definite place to meet his girls. It was at the entrance to the Longchamps Racetrack, located in the park. Although meeting them this way exposed him to some risk from the police, he chalked it up as a business hazard. Whenever he was picked up, which happened occasionally, he was always back on the street within a couple of days.

He parked the Renault next to the darkened entrance and checked the time on the new watch he had bought at Cartier's only one week ago. He had paid a lot for it, but it was worth it to him. The envious looks from his friends more than made up for the price.

He had arrived with a minute or two to spare. He lighted a cigarette and almost at the same time saw one of girls walking toward his car. He rolled down the window on the passenger side and waited.

While she was a few feet away, she called out his name. "Armand, is that you?"

"Damn it," he snapped as she came up to the door. "How many times must I tell you not to use my name. Get in the car."

As she got in next to him, he rolled down the window on his side and flipped the cigarette into the road. "How much?"

he asked. Experience had taught him to greet his girls this way. If he waited for them to tell him, they would always lie and try to cheat him out of his money.

She fumbled in her purse, bringing out a thin stack of bills.

"How much?" he demanded again.

"Enough." The man's voice startled Armand. He jerked his head around toward the window next to him. Looking in was Police Inspector Antoine Duval. Behind Duval there was another police officer.

"Well, Armand," Duval continued. "How's business?"

"*Merde,*" Boucher muttered. He knew he was in for a long morning. He didn't mind paying the bail and certain fine. What he minded most was the hassle.

"All right, now what?" he asked the inspector. Of course, he knew very well what would happen. The panier à salade, the paddy wagon, would be along soon to collect him and the girl. He didn't want the other girl to show up and be taken as well. If she did, it would become an expensive day for him. He sneered at Duval.

"I'm ready to go whenever you are." He was very composed. He had gone through it enough times to know everything that would take place.

Two hours later Armand Boucher had lost all his composure. He was talking with Inspector Marcel Mercier, from the Central Office for Frauds and Counterfeits. Mercier had come to the police station at the request of Duval, who had thought there was something strange about the American dollars in Boucher's pocket.

"Come, Boucher." Mercier said. "Are you trying to tell me you collected this money from one of your girls?" He pointed to the hundred-dollar bills lying on a table between him and Boucher.

"I swear to you I did."

"Bah. Your sluts don't make that kind of money. No, Boucher, I'll tell you about this money. You're passing it for a ring of counterfeiters, buying it at a discount perhaps. That's where it comes from."

"I swear it came from customers, American customers," Boucher replied. He appeared very frightened.

Mercier turned to Duval. "Lock him up. We have enough on him here to put him away for a long time."

Duval, who had been in on the interrogation from the start, signaled to a policeman. The policeman escorted Boucher from the office.

Boucher had not told where he had gotten the money because he did not want his apartment operation known to the police. Now, just before the door was closed behind him, he called out, "Wait, I'll tell you where I got it."

He was brought back to his chair. At once he explained about the American giving him the money. "Damn American thief," he complained. "Imagine giving me counterfeit money."

When he had finished talking he was removed from the office. Mercier explained to Duval that these hundreds looked like the same stuff that had recently begun to infiltrate France. Already, since the first bill had shown up, the Central Office had close to seven thousand dollars of it. Now they could add this five hundred to the collection.

Duval asked when the first bill had shown up and got a wide grin from Mercier. "Two days ago. The market's been flooded with it. This is the first break we've had in the case."

Swift plans were made to raid the apartment on Avenue de Villiers. With a little luck the Americans would still be there. It was just after four in the morning.

At the apartment, the police found only one girl, Hélène Colbert. She explained that everyone else had left about half an hour earlier. She couldn't tell the police anything about the Americans as she spoke no English and did not get involved in any conversations.

The only useful information they got from her was the address of one of the other girls, who did speak English.

"She may know where the Americans are staying because she spoke to several of them," Hélène told Mercier.

Duval and Mercier went to the address of the girl,

Madeleine Durand. She had just gone to bed and was not cooperative until told she might spend the rest of the day in a cell. She changed her attitude quickly. Yes, she did speak English. Yes, she knew the name of the man she had been with and where he was staying. His name was Venner and he was in a hotel on Rue de Berri. She named the hotel for the two police officers.

Mercier and Duval woke Venner up. When they identified themselves, Venner began by denying that he had been in the apartment with the girls.

"I don't know what the hell you guys are talking about. If you don't clear out of here I'll call my embassy."

Mercier, in good English, suggested to Venner that he might well want to call the embassy. "You're in serious trouble, Mr. Venner."

Duval asked if Venner had any more hundred-dollar bills. He explained about the ones they had taken from the pimp, Boucher.

When Venner digested this, he quieted down at once. He showed them his passport and told them he was a high-ranking business executive and that they could and should check him out quickly as he didn't want to get mixed up in something like this. Yes, he said, he did have two more hundred-dollar bills, and he produced them. It was impossible that the money was no good, he explained, as he had gotten all the bills from his bank in Dallas.

Mercier took a look at the money and assured Venner that they were, like the others, counterfeits. It was arranged that Venner would remain in the hotel until he was checked and cleared.

By midafternoon the police were satisfied that Venner had nothing to do with the bad money. It had now become time to try to track down the source in the United States. The agency to do that was the National Central Bureau, Interpol-France.

The normal method for requesting information from another country is by dispatch letter. In this case, however, it was felt that time was too important a factor. At the rate the money was being spread around, even a day extra could be expensive. The source had to be found and choked off quickly.

A telex was sent to the Treasury Department, Interpol-United States. The telex contained all the information the French had at that time. A duplicate copy of the telex was filed with the General Secretariat in St. Cloud. The message was sent at four in the afternoon French time, ten in the morning in Washington.

The time difference between France and the United States was working for the police. From Washington, an Interpol agent was put on a plane for Dallas. A warning call to the bank kept the president and three assistants waiting for the arrival of the agent.

The Interpol man, Harry Tremont, was an expert in false money. He was met at the airport by a city detective, Walter Richardson. They raced to the bank.

Tremont had two ideas, both of them admittedly long shots. The first was to examine the hundred-dollar bills in the bank vault. There might be a possibility of finding more of the counterfeits. The trouble with that idea was that the normal movement of money in and out of a bank and transfers of cash would have probably moved out the false notes. As he expected, they did not find any more of the bills.

Three more bank employees were summoned from their homes while Tremont and the others were checking the vault. These people were put to work going over deposits made within a three-day period before Venner had withdrawn his money. It was also a slim chance, but this one paid off.

After four hours' steady work, three deposit slips that could have contained the hundreds were unearthed. Now, more police were called in. Going in pairs they went to see the depositors. Tremont went with Richardson to a bar on Mockingbird Lane. It was agreed that all the pairs would meet back at the bank to exchange information.

Tremont and Richardson returned first. Tremont had the information he needed. The owner of the bar he had visited remembered taking in seven hundred dollars in hundreds.

"Seven of them. Sure I remember," he had said to Tremont. "Who wouldn't remember a guy handing you money like that. He'd owed it to me a long time. It was a gambling debt."

When the other police showed up Tremont was able to give them the name and address of the man who'd turned the money in to the bar.

While waiting for the other four policemen, Richardson had called in to request a check on the name they had, a David Holliday. He received a negative answer. There was nothing in the Dallas police files on any David Holliday.

An unmarked car was used to drive to Holliday's home in North Dallas. It was ten minutes before midnight when Tremont and the police knocked on the front door.

Holliday, an insurance-company executive, readily admitted paying his debt with the bills. He had received them from a neighbor, who lived three houses away in the same block. The money was for a car he'd sold this man, named James Duncan.

The group left and went to Duncan's house. After waking Duncan up and explaining the nature of their call, they were told that he too had received the money in a car deal.

"As a matter of fact, I got the money the day before I bought Holliday's car. It's a hobby of mine, fixing up older cars and selling them. Profitable hobby, too."

He had sold a car, he explained, to a Paul Chase. He gave the police Chase's address. It was an apartment complex not far from Duncan's house.

And now the hunt came to an end. Paul Chase was not home. The manager of the complex was awakened. He told Tremont that Chase was on a business trip. "If you want to speak to Mr. Chase, you'll have to go to Hong Kong."

The manager wasn't exactly certain what Chase's business was, but he thought Chase and another man owned an import company.

"Lucky guy," he said. "He's always off somewhere. Must be a good business to be in, I guess."

Chapter 8

Daylight broke over Dallas. It was Friday, January 24, and Tremont had not been to bed. He called Washington and gave them a rundown of all his information from Richardson's office.

Washington contacted the General Secretariat and also sent a telex to the May House, Police Headquarters, Arsenal Street, in Hong Kong, the National Central Bureau of that busy and crowded city.

Washington sent the message at ten-fifteen in the morning and because of the time difference between the two cities, it was eleven-fifteen in the evening of the same day in Hong Kong.

The Hong Kong Police did not lose any time. They were able to place Paul Chase at his hotel within ten minutes of receiving the message. The truth was, they had also been lucky. It was the first hotel they had checked. Chase was sitting by himself in the hotel bar when the police arrived.

Detective-Inspector Bryan Smith slid into a seat across from Paul Chase, who was in a booth. He introduced himself and looked over his shoulder quickly to see if his two men were posted at the bar entrance, which they were.

Chase was a large man with a meaty round face and close cropped gray hair. If he was at all surprised by Smith's sudden appearance, he gave no indication of it.

After explaining to Chase that the United States was interested in finding out where he had gotten the hundred-dollars bills, Smith asked if Chase had any more with him.

This brought a surprised reaction. "That's a strange request. I may have some hundreds with me, I'm not sure."

"Would you mind looking, please?" Smith asked.

"Now?" Chase's tone changed from surprise to annoyance.

"Why don't you come back in the morning? I'm not going anywhere."

"Please look now," Smith directed.

Chase reached inside his jacket and brought out a billfold. He thumbed through it and then shook his head. "Don't have any."

Smith did not like the way the American had looked in the billfold. He reached out his hand. "May I?"

Chase put the billfold back in his pocket. "Not without a search warrant."

"You're only complicating things, Mr. Chase," Smith said. "Please remember you're here in this city as a guest. We can ask you to leave Hong Kong if we wish."

Sullenly, Chase handed over the billford. He lit a cigarette while Smith went through it.

"What's this?" Smith asked. He held up a bill folded into fourths. He undid it and flattened it out on the table.

"It looks like money," Chase answered testily.

"Yes. A hundred-dollar bill, Mr. Chase. I'm sorry, but you'll have to come along with me. There are some things we need to discuss."

"I didn't see it when I looked," Chase said angrily. "I forgot I had it." He slammed his hand down on the table. "I'm a businessman, and I've got business tonight."

"You'll have to take care of it in the morning," Smith told him.

In an office at the Arsenal Street police station, Chase sat facing Smith and explained in outraged tones that he did not have to answer any questions.

Smith, continuing his polite manner, told Chase once again that it was important that he remember where he got the hundred-dollar bills he had paid to Duncan in Dallas.

At two in the morning, Chase decided to answer Smith's question. "All right. I got those hundreds from a guy I do business with sometimes. He lives in Dallas. He bought some merchandise from me and paid me in cash."

"Why didn't you say so earlier?"

"Because I don't like being asked a lot of stupid questions. Because I have some rights. I haven't done anything wrong, and I know it."

"Why don't you give us the name of this man, Mr. Chase. We'll pass the information along, and you can go back to your hotel and get some sleep."

"I don't know his name," Chase said. His moon face was very red.

"I thought you said he was a customer."

"He is. All I know is he pays cash. You understand what I mean?"

Smith asked if Chase meant he was doing illegal business with the man. He received an affirmative nod, and then with some irritation Chase explained that he hadn't wanted to go into this because he was cheating his partner in the import store in Texas. He gave Smith the name of the man.

"His name's Charley Stevens. I've been dealing with him for a few years. He's listed in the phone book. He'll verify what I told you about getting the money from him."

This information was sent to Interpol-Washington at once. Although the date was now January 25 in Hong Kong, it was still January 24 in the United States. Agent Tremont, waiting in Dallas, was given the new information and told to investigate.

Tremont had managed to sneak in an hour's sleep in Detective Richardson's office. Now, bleary-eyed, he and Richardson located Stevens' address and drove there.

Charley Stevens lived in a modern high-rise apartment in Oak Cliff, a suburb of Dallas. He was watching television when his two visitors arrived.

Tremont asked if Stevens knew Paul Chase. The question seemed to upset Stevens. He was a short thin man with a twitch at the right corner of his mouth. He admitted he knew Chase, that sometimes he did business with Chase.

"Why?" Stevens wanted to know. "What's he done?" The twitch at the corner of his mouth was working frantically.

Tremont then asked if Stevens recalled giving Chase a cash

payment in hundred-dollar bills. At this, Stevens seemed to shrivel up. He looked about the room as if seeking a place to escape.

"You better tell us about that money," Tremont suggested.

"There's something wrong with it," Stevens said. "That's why you're here. I knew it, I knew it would happen."

"Where did you get it from?" Tremont asked.

"I thought it was bad money when I took it." Stevens sounded confused. "Not when I took it right away. Later, the next day. I was looking at it and thought it didn't look right. I didn't want to turn it in and lose it all. I gave it to Chase because I knew he was planning a trip to the Far East and thought he might lose it over there."

"Where did it come from?" Tremont asked again.

Stevens told the agent that he had been given the money in payment for some goods he had sold to a man in Oklahoma City named Robert Baxter.

At eleven-thirty that same night, Tremont and a detective, Malcolm Reese, from the Oklahoma City Police, were inside Baxter's house. Baxter was a known police character with a record dating back to 1965. He had recently served one year in the Oklahoma State Penitentiary for a forged check. His present business was selling used and new merchandise at state and county fairs.

When confronted by Tremont and Reese he denied giving Stevens any money. "I barely know the guy. Seen him around once or twice at the fairs, so help me, that's all."

"You know how long you can get locked up for if you have anything to do with passing bad money?" Reese asked.

Baxter shrugged. "I ain't done nothing."

"I'm going to take you in on suspicion," Reese said. "Then we'll get a deposition from Stevens. And then . . ."

"Okay, okay," Baxter said. "Will you guys help me if I level?"

"No promises," Tremont said. "If you help us we'll say that you did when you go to court."

Baxter licked his lips. "I made a buy on that stuff, about two thousand dollars."

"Who makes it?" Tremont had little hope of a positive answer but the question cost nothing.

"I don't know. I only made a deal for it at 20 percent."

The questioning continued, and Baxter talked freely. He had bought the money from a man in Dallas, Albert Grogan. He explained that Grogan owned a bar on Greenville Avenue but would not sell the counterfeit money there. To buy, it was necessary to go to Grogan's home.

Tremont was weary when the session came to an end. He left Baxter in Reese's custody and headed back to Dallas. First, however, he called Washington and brought them up to date. He also called Detective Richardson in Dallas to let him know what time he'd be arriving. In reply to Richardson's question as to whether he had managed to get any sleep yet, Tremont laughed. It was now January 25 in Dallas, Texas, as well as in Washington, D.C.

•

At ten in the evening, Paul Chase ate a steak dinner in his hotel restaurant. The incident with the police had caused him to miss a business appointment. He hadn't been lying to Smith. He had had to catch up on that appointment during the day while still making his other scheduled meetings. Smith had told him earlier that evening that his problems were over. The police had verified his story in Dallas. Despite the politeness of the Hong Kong Police, Chase was anxious to return to the United States. He had two more days of business meetings before he could go home. It had been extremely uncomfortable for him to be involved with the police in a strange place.

•

At about the same time that Paul Chase cut into his first slice of steak, Tremont and Richardson knocked on the door of a house in South Dallas. It was early in the morning, January 25, and Tremont looked, in his own words, "like an army had marched over me." However, for what he had in mind, he preferred to look that way.

The door was opened by a man in red flannel pajamas.

Tremont hadn't seen those in years and suppressed a chuckle. He asked if the man were Al Grogan.

Although it was obvious that the man they were speaking to was still sleepy, they also noticed that he had very alert eyes. Tremont thought him formidable. He appeared to be somewhere in the neighborhood of 275 pounds, and he towered over the agent, who was six feet tall himself.

The man admitted his name was Grogan, then at once asked what the two men wanted. His tone was decidedly unfriendly.

Tremont explained that Baxter had told them to look up Grogan in Dallas.

"I don't know no Baxter," Grogan said.

"From Oklahoma City," Tremont said.

Grogan said he never went there and didn't know anyone living there.

"I want to buy some of your merchandise," Tremont told him.

Grogan, in surly tones, explained that he didn't know what they wanted to buy and that he had nothing for sale.

Tremont said that he had different information, and he had five thousand dollars that he wanted to spend with Grogan.

Grogan looked them over suspiciously, then, seeming to make up his mind, invited them into the house. They stepped through the doorway into a messy living room.

Grogan immediately asked them for a description of Baxter. He listened intently while Tremont described both Baxter and his house. Evidently Grogan was satisfied. He admitted he had some counterfeit money and that it was high quality. He offered to sell it at 25 percent of its value.

Tremont looked at Richardson, who nodded, then Tremont asked Grogan to show him the money. "Let's see it," he said.

"Let's see the cash first," Grogan replied.

"Oh, no," Tremont told him. "I want to see if you have enough for me to spend five big ones. If you can't handle that kind of action I don't want to deal."

"I'll tell you what I'll do," Grogan offered. "I'll let you have a peek at the stuff, enough of a peek so you can see its quality. Then you show me what you're carrying and we'll make the deal."

Tremont and Richardson agreed, and Grogan disappeared into another room. He returned with three one-hundred-dollar bills. "Here," he said. "Look at this."

Richardson pulled out his pistol. "And you look at this. You're under arrest."

Grogan stared at them in disbelief, then let out a roar of anger.

"Relax and sit down over there," Richardson ordered, motioning with the revolver.

Grogan sat in the center of his lumpy couch. "Oh, hell, this is going to cost me." He looked from Tremont to Richardson. "What kind of a deal can I make?"

"No deals, but if you cooperate we'll put in a good word for you," Tremont said.

Richardson, still holding his gun on Grogan, was using the phone to request a car to take Grogan to jail. At the same time, Grogan was evidently giving some thought to what Tremont had said.

"Okay," he finally said. "I'll tell you what I can."

"Is it made in the city?" Richardson demanded.

"No. It's made in Hong Kong."

An alarm went off in Tremont's head. "You know a guy named Paul Chase?"

Grogan nodded. "Sure. He's the one that brings it in."

•

Detective Smith got the urgent call at his home exactly one hour after he had gone to bed. He looked at the clock while he dressed. It was one in the morning on January 26. He was standing outside his house at the moment that the police car pulled up, two officers inside.

They made good time, coming from Smith's house on the Repulse Bay side of Hong Kong to the downtown hotel that Chase was staying in.

Chase opened his door in response to the knocking. When he saw the expression on Smith's face and the two uniformed policemen behind him, he groaned.

"You're under arrest," Smith told him.

"I know," Chase answered.

With sweat running down his moon face, Chase told Smith that the money was, indeed, made in Hong Kong. He gave Smith the address and a name.

Smith ordered another car to take Chase in to the police station, and then he and one of the policemen went to the address Chase had supplied.

While driving to the Ventris Road address, a check was made on the ownership of the house. It was discovered that, although owned by a Chinese banker, the house had been rented out as income property. Ventris Road was high over the city with a view of the harbor and the Kowloon side. Most of the buildings were high-rise apartments, but there were a few private homes squeezed between the tall apartment buildings.

The police car parked in front of one of these houses. There was a wall around it and a gate in the wall. Smith and the policeman walked through the gate and up to the door. Lights were still on. Smith rang the bell.

When the door opened, Smith found himself looking at a man of middle age with a short trim beard. The detective identified himself and entered the house. The man introduced himself as Harvey Carmody, an American. He didn't seem disturbed by the presence of the police at that hour.

Carmody explained he was using the house for a couple of weeks. It belonged to a man named John Peabody, who at the moment was in Tokyo on business. Carmody was an old friend of Peabody's and would stay on about a week more after Peabody returned. He said he expected Peabody to come back in three or four more days.

Smith asked if Carmody would be good enough to show him some identification. Carmody produced an American passport.

Smith looked it over. "Thanks very much, Mr. Peabody."

"No, no," Carmody laughed. "I'm Carmody."

"Yes, Mr. Carmody/Peabody, you're under arrest," Smith said.

The color drained from the man's face. Then he shrugged. "What you're looking for is in the basement."

"I know," Smith replied. "Chase told us everything."

•

In the basement of the house the police found the press and the plates used to make the counterfeit money. In addition, they discovered a million and a half dollars, counterfeit, packed in boxes in a closet.

Harvey Carmody/Peabody and Paul Chase were extradited to the United States. They stood trial in the Federal District Court of Northern Texas, along with Albert Grogan.

Chase and Carmody were convicted and sentenced to fifteen years' imprisonment each. Albert Grogan received a five-year term. All three are serving their sentences in the Federal Penitentiary at Atlanta, Georgia.

Robert Baxter, who was on parole, was sent back to the Oklahoma State Penitentiary to finish his sentence. There is a federal detainer waiting for him when he is released.

Charles Stevens was put on federal probation for one year.

In France, Antonio Risko, an Italian national, Manuel Castillo, a Spanish national, Ludwig Bremer, a German national, and Franz Schliff, also a German national, were arrested in connection with the case and charged with knowingly passing counterfeit money. They are all serving prison terms in France.

Interpol entered the case on January 23. The final arrest was made on January 28.

Chapter 9

One of the corner offices on the sixth floor of Interpol Headquarters in St. Cloud looks out over the Seine to a sweeping view of Paris. From the window it's possible to see Sacré-Coeur's white dome in Montmartre, the Arc de Triomphe at Place de l'Étoile, the Tour Eiffel, and the new high-rise buildings that are changing the skyline of Paris.

If the view is magnificent, the office itself is austere. There is a minimum of furniture, all of which is utilitarian: a desk, a few chairs, and a metal closet that doubles as a filing cabinet and a place to hang coats. The furniture is at a minimum here, but the workload is always at a maximum, for this is the private office of the Interpol department chief whose responsibilities are concerned with crimes of violence and thefts.

This man is also a commissaire in the French Police. Before joining Interpol he earned a law degree from Grenoble University, then attended the École Nationale Supérieure de Police to gain his appointment as a police commissaire, and served three years with the immigration authorities in Le Havre. He is fluent in French, English, and Spanish, the official working languages of Interpol.

In the four years he has worked with Interpol, he has had an intensive exposure to worldwide crime. Naturally enough, during this time he has formed some theories and opinions especially oriented toward violent crime and theft.

As do his colleagues at Interpol, he thinks the crime rate is rising alarmingly. Last year, Interpol was involved with 309 crimes of violence against persons and about 2,000 thefts. The previous year, the figures were 200 crimes of violence and 1,200 cases of theft. The year before that it was proportionately less.

He mentioned two main reasons for the mounting statistics. First is the general apathy of people toward violence. There has been too much shown graphically on television, too much reported accurately in newspapers, and too much described in detail by other media. Who is going to get overly excited about one murder when with a twist of a dial it's possible to see hundreds butchered? The total effect has been to remove the shock of maiming and death. To compound the situation, the details of various crimes are sufficiently explained so that the most obtuse moron knows how to duplicate what he has seen.

This combination, exposure and explanation, has in turn led many an enthusiastic amateur to try his hand at violent crime. This type of person, tending to panic in the course of his actions, often will hurt someone.

Murder, once a highly personal type crime in the sense that it was most often committed by people intimate with one another, has now become a simple expediency; the logical conclusion to a robbery, rape, or kidnapping.

There is one major area of crime where violent acts are at a minimum. Thefts, of all kinds, rarely include violence.

Pickpockets, those sleight-of-hand artists whose activities have plagued both public and police for many centuries, are thriving as never before. Operating in family groups, the younger members taught by the older, these criminals follow the crowds. They can be found at major sporting events, conventions, and, thanks to ease of modern travel, almost all large tourist centers. For them, documents such as passports and identity cards are as valuable as plain cash. There is a ready market for official documents in the underworld.

Art thieves are also enjoying a gilt-edged era. Prices are higher now for works of art as the appeal of investing in art rather than fluctuating securities has brought a new group of affluent buyers to the marketplace.

Stolen art, except for particularly famous objects, can be sold through legitimate houses to legitimate buyers. It may take some time for the work to reach a legitimate house, but that is where it usually ends up. After passing through many hands, aided by false papers of origin, it goes on the market.

The big problem for Interpol and other agencies is the loose control over documentation. They are working on this problem.

Another flourishing business involves smuggling human beings from one country to another. This racket is particularly vicious since the victims arrive in the new country in virtual bondage. Poor, mostly illiterate, and unable to speak the new language, they work at menial labor and pay most of their earnings to the smugglers. They are afraid to contact the authorities because of their illegal entry and so continue, sometimes for years, subsisting and paying until caught and deported. The smugglers are the type of criminal who at other times smuggles anything of value. With many countries experiencing vast unemployment, the smuggler has turned his attention to exploiting the human opportunities. This kind of crime is taking up more and more of Interpol's time.

One crime on the decrease is jewel theft. That is to say, the sophisticated jewel thief pictured so dramatically in movies and literature is becoming a thing of the past. Thefts of jewelry still occur, of course, but today jewels are stolen at the point of a gun more often than not, putting it into the realm of armed robbery.

And armed robbery is probably the fastest-rising crime. Everyone seems to be able to get his hands on a gun these days, and robbery seems to be the most popular use for it. This does not mean that the new wave of amateurs has pushed the professionals out of business. They have only swelled the statistics. The tough professional still exists, the kind who doesn't mind putting a bullet into someone just to see how big a hole his bullet makes. Not long ago, Interpol hunted a man like that.

·

Léon LaFarge, thirty-five years old, had most of his life's history, at least his adult history, on record with the French police. He had been arrested no fewer than twenty-three times on various charges, including extortion, armed robbery, assault, pimping, dealing in narcotics, and murder.

Only one conviction had been secured from all these

arrests. An extortion charge cost LaFarge three years in a French prison. He was released in June 1974 and immediately went back to his old habits.

The police were aware of what he was doing but had nothing solid enough to arrest him. That did not discourage them from keeping an eye on him. They were certain he would eventually give them a reason to put him away for a long time and wanted to be ready when it happened.

LaFarge affected the style of his idea of an American gangster. He always dressed in a black suit, black shoes, yellow shirt, and black tie. If anyone was inclined to laugh at this outfit, one look at his face changed his mind.

He had a long face, accentuated by a heavy hooknose. He combed his hair straight back from his forehead without a part. His eyes, widely spaced from the hooknose, were normally narrowed suspiciously. His mouth was small and unsmiling, the lips thin and bloodless.

LaFarge was close to six feet tall and extremely muscular. He had a well-deserved reputation for physical strength, and his one joke appeared to be related to it. He liked showing his physical power by lifting up a man of his own weight by holding him under the arms and hoisting him high in the air.

In August 1974, the police got a lead from an informer that LaFarge was going to make a deal for three kilos of heroin. The transaction was to take place in a Montparnasse night club known to the police as a favorite hangout for LaFarge and other racketeers.

A special squad of five police officers under the supervision of a chief inspector named Christian Raymond filtered into the club in plainclothes on the night of Wednesday, August 14. Their informer had told them that at exactly one in the morning LaFarge would be making his deal.

It was easy to spot LaFarge in the club. He sat at a table, dressed in his usual style, surrounded by his cronies. The police knew these people but kept their interested looks on LaFarge.

There was a large and noisy crowd in the club. Except for a few tourists who had wandered in, almost all the customers were known or suspected criminals. It was that kind of place.

As the hands of a clock near the front door moved to one, LaFarge rose from his table and walked toward the toilets located in the rear of the night club. There were two: one for men and one for women, side by side, each door marked by a black silhouette to distinguish who was welcome.

When LaFarge made his move toward the toilets, Raymond and another inspector, Jean Ricard, got up and followed, slowly so as not to alarm LaFarge.

There was a man waiting for LaFarge at the toilets, later identified as a Spanish national, Fernando Torres. He was carrying a plastic shopping bag in his hand, the type given out by department stores with the store name printed on both sides.

As LaFarge opened the door to the men's room and stepped inside, Torres followed. Raymond motioned with his hand to Ricard and the two police officers raced to the door and burst through it, surprising LaFarge and Torres, who were examining the contents of the plastic bag.

"Drop that bag and stand against the wall," Raymond ordered, gun in hand.

LaFarge and Torres obeyed the order, while Ricard, who also had drawn his revolver, looked in the bag. "Only a pair of shoes in here," he told Raymond.

Raymond looked at the two men, then said to Ricard, "Search them."

Ricard holstered his gun and moved first toward Torres. As he did so, he stepped directly in front of Inspector Raymond. It was a fatal error.

Later, Ricard was to explain what happened next. "Suddenly," he said, "I saw a pistol in LaFarge's hand. Before I could react, he'd fired twice very rapidly. The first bullet caught me in the shoulder and I was flung to the wall against the urinals. The second bullet hit me in the belly. I remained conscious although unable to move and saw Inspector Raymond's face disintegrate. He must have been shot squarely in the face. I passed out then but not before hearing two more shots."

In fact, LaFarge had hit Raymond in the face with his first shot and had then fired two more bullets into the now dead inspector.

Outside the toilet, the three other police officers had grouped close to the doors when they saw Raymond and Ricard go inside. When they heard the shots, they instinctively moved for the door, but another shot splintered through the door and the slug caught one of them in the throat, killing him instantly. The two remaining officers hesitated, afraid to fire into the toilet for fear of hitting one of their own, yet at the same time convinced that LaFarge was in control behind the door.

They knelt over the fallen man, Inspector Blanchard, unaware that he was already dead, while trying to decide what to do next. In the club, surprisingly few people were aware of what had happened. The music blaring from a jukebox and the high level of noise in general may have screened the shots from most ears.

Those people sitting at tables from which the toilet doors were visible were the only ones who had an idea of what was taking place. They began moving for the exits, spreading confusion as they rushed and bumped past other customers. Quickly the news got around, and panic took over. There was a wild scramble to get out of the club.

The two officers outside the toilet door huddled together, guns drawn but not sure of what to do next. Inside the toilet, LaFarge, certain he had killed both Raymond and Ricard, was busy forcing open the window over the double sinks. Torres, in a state of shock, watched LaFarge without helping him. LaFarge ignored him, concentrating on what he was doing.

Finally, after what seemed like a long time to the dazed Torres but was probably not more than two minutes, LaFarge was ready to climb through the window. He turned to Torres, shoved the muzzle of his revolver under Torres' nose and pulled the trigger. Nothing happened. The gun was out of bullets. LaFarge stared at Torres a couple of seconds longer, then jammed the gun in his belt and climbed out the window.

And now Torres reacted. He screamed that he was alone

and unarmed although at that moment he did not know there were police outside the door.

At his cries, the two officers moved into the toilet and took in the situation. Torres, as soon as he saw them with their guns, raised his hands. He backed up against the sinks, repeating over and over that he had had no part in the shooting.

Ricard lay crumpled between a urinal and the wall, one arm draped over a water pipe, the other in his lap. The lower part of his shirt and the top of his pants were red with his blood. He was barely alive.

Raymond was on his back at a right angle to the urinals. His face looked as if it had been chopped open with a meat cleaver. His exposed shirt front was bloody. He was so obviously dead that the officers immediately went to Ricard. They knew Raymond was past any help.

While waiting for the ambulance, Torres was questioned. He was too rattled to give a coherent story. The officers, noticing the open window, realized how LaFarge had escaped. One of them stayed with Torres, the other pushed past the crowd of curiosity seekers and made his way around the corner of the block to get to the alley that was behind the club. There was no trace of LaFarge by this time.

As more police descended upon the scene, a call went in describing the first details to the Ministry of Interior. A citywide alert for LaFarge began. He had about a twenty-minute head start on the police.

The first order of business was to block all exits from Paris. Men were posted at bridges that connected Paris to the suburbs. Roadblocks were set up on the auto routes. Police were posted at the airports, railroad terminals, and bus stations. A net had been spread around the city. When the last post had called in to say it was in position, it was one hour and twenty minutes since LaFarge had left the club. The time was two-thirty in the morning. Paris was sealed.

The remainder of the night passed all too quickly for the police. At six in the morning, suspecting LaFarge had either slipped out before the police had been posted or had somehow gotten through the net, a national alert was put into effect. The same procedure that had taken place in Paris now took place throughout France. Major highways, airports, ports, and railroads were alerted. Police in every department of France were on the lookout for the killer.

At nine in the morning, it was decided to continue the total alert in Paris in case LaFarge had found a hiding place within the city. Squads were organized to check every place he was known to have frequented. In addition, a search began to find everyone with whom LaFarge was known to associate. Every lead was to be checked out.

By noon, with nothing in on LaFarge, a directive was issued to maintain the net around Paris for the rest of the day and through the coming night. After that, the cordon would have to be called off. Traffic was getting jammed up on the roads, and complaints about police harassment were pouring into the Ministry of Interior.

At three in the afternoon, the story was released to the press. At four-thirty in the afternoon, it had become a triple murder. Ricard, after regaining consciouness in the hospital early in the morning and telling his version of the events, had relapsed and died in the intensive-care unit.

Torres, under maximum security, had been able to tell what he'd observed. He explained that the shoes he had taken into the toilet in the plastic bag had been for the purpose of identifying him to LaFarge. The actual transfer of the heroin was to have taken place later and not in the club.

"Why, then," the police asked, "if there were no narcotics on the scene, had LaFarge thought it necessary to shoot his way out?"

Torres couldn't supply the answer to that question. LaFarge had the answer, and he was nowhere in sight.

Chapter 10

LaFarge was not in Paris. He had traveled during the night and was in Lyon, hidden by a friend in a small room over a garage.

After going through the toilet window, he had run down the alley behind the club to the street, found a taxi, and ordered the driver to take him to Versailles. Minutes after leaving the taxi in Versailles, he had stolen a Mercedes sedan and driven to Lyon, arriving just before seven in the morning. He had managed to get into the city before all the roadblocks were in place.

The Mercedes was hidden in the garage, minus its plates, its body covered with blankets. LaFarge's friend, René Perier, was known to the police. They had a case against him for dealing in narcotics. Unknown to LaFarge, Perier was at liberty only because he had agreed to be an informer for the police.

LaFarge made a deal with Perier, explaining he had shot his way out of the Paris club and needed to leave the country. He offered Perier four thousand dollars to help him—two thousand in advance, the rest as he would be leaving France. He needed to be hidden and fed, to be taken to Marseilles, and to get passage booked for Lisbon.

Perier agreed eagerly for two reasons. First, he wanted the money. Second, he saw a good chance to get rid of the police charges. He thought if he turned LaFarge in the police would be grateful enough to drop their case against him. At the same time, he knew he would have to be careful. LaFarge wouldn't hesitate to kill him, and he knew it. His plan was to go ahead and do what LaFarge asked, get the balance of the money, and only when he had seen LaFarge aboard a ship would he go to the police. There was always the chance that if he turned

LaFarge in sooner LaFarge might get free and come after him. Waiting until LaFarge was on the ship would cover up the fact that he had marked him to the police. At least that's what Perier thought.

The two men decided to let a week go by before taking any action. During that week LaFarge would remain hidden in the room, and Perier would make the necessary arrangements. He had to get not only passage for LaFarge but also false papers: a passport and identity card.

LaFarge wanted to get out of France quickly. He knew the police would continue to look for him in France for a two- or three-month period before looking outside the country. In that time he would be able to set himself up safely in another country. He didn't tell Perier where he planned to go after reaching Lisbon.

In three days, Perier had supplied LaFarge with the false documents. The new name LaFarge would be using was Jacques Rollain. If LaFarge was glad to get his hands on the passport and identity card, he was just as glad to hear that a Greek freighter would be leaving Marseilles for Lisbon on Thursday, August 22. Perier had done a good job. He had, with very short notice, booked passage for LaFarge.

LaFarge spent his time in the little room reading about himself in the newspapers and playing solitaire. He chafed at the confinement and, according to Perier, seemed to get increasingly suspicious about Perier's actions.

Because they were not certain of the exact time the freighter would dock or leave Marseilles, it was necessary to keep in constant contact with the freight agent in Marseilles. The freighter was scheduled to be in port only one day. The plan was that once they knew the ship had arrived, they would drive to the port, getting there at night just before sailing time. Perier would use a small truck, and LaFarge would be concealed in a wooden crate. The papers providing LaFarge with passage would also permit the truck to be driven close to the ship, at which time, under cover of darkness, LaFarge could safely get out of his crate and go on board.

On the twenty-second, the scheduled docking date, the freight agent informed Perier that the ship would be a day late. In fact, it was two days late, not docking until ten in the morning on Saturday, August 24.

Perier timed his drive to Marseilles so that they got there an hour before sailing time, scheduled for eleven at night. He drove with a warning from LaFarge that if anything happened to make them miss the boat, he would be shot.

As Perier drove through central Marseilles, killing a little time, he almost had an accident on the Rue du Théâtre Français when a sports car cut across in front of him, making him jam on the brakes to avoid a collision. He said afterward that his only thought at the time was that LaFarge would kill him. He drove with shaking hands the rest of the way.

Perier parked the truck in the shadow of a warehouse on the pier, some two hundred yards from the freighter. When he was certain it was safe, he opened the loosely fastened wooden crate and let LaFarge out. LaFarge didn't say anything about the lurching stop Perier had made earlier to avoid the collision. He simply walked to the cab of the truck and slid into the seat.

Perier joined him, sitting behind the wheel, and waited for his two thousand dollars. He had decided that he would wait until the ship cleared port before contacting the police. LaFarge would be in for a nasty shock when the ship docked again.

LaFarge was dressed in work clothes. He had a small suitcase with additional clothing that Perier had supplied. Now, as they sat together in the cab of the small truck, he turned to Perier.

"You did a good job," LaFarge said. "Here's your payoff."

It wasn't money that LaFarge had in his hand. It was a revolver. "I can't take any chances," he told Perier. He fired twice. The bullets slammed into Perier's chest. LaFarge left the truck and walked to the ship. He was certain René Perier was dead.

Perier was not dead. He was very badly wounded and losing a lot of blood. He had no strength to move although he tried desperately to sound the truck horn. He said he thought if he could even fall across the horn he might have a chance to live. He didn't know the strength of his own constitution.

He was found by a night watchman just as the freighter left. He was in a coma and was to remain comatose for ten days before coming out of it and recovering enough to tell the police about LaFarge.

Of course, it was far too late. By that time Léon LaFarge, or Jacques Rollain, as his new passport stated, was in Buenos Aires. He had chosen that city because he knew someone there, someone who could help him. The man he went to see was known as Paul Sèvres. His business was narcotics, and he welcomed LaFarge like a long lost cousin, which is exactly what he was.

.

With Perier's disclosure that LaFarge had gone to Lisbon, the French Police turned to Interpol.

A red notice, with photograph, fingerprints, and the arrest warrant for murder, was circulated among the member nations. The fact that LaFarge was using the alias Jacques Rollain was included.

The National Central Bureau-Portugal quickly turned up LaFarge's entry into their country as well as his departure date and destination.

In Buenos Aires, the Policia Federal Argentina, Direcion de Investigaciones, the National Central Bureau there, verified through immigration that a Jacques Rollain had indeed entered the country.

It now appeared that LaFarge was trapped. The police began a check on all hotel registrations dating back three full weeks. They began their hunt on September 11, 1974. They were one day too late. LaFarge had left Buenos Aires on Wednesday, September 10, by plane. His destination was Chicago.

He also had a new name for the trip, along with a new forged passport. His new alias was Henri Villemain. His business in Chicago was to set up a contact that could serve as a distribution point for narcotics coming in from Argentina.

Because of his fluency in English, LaFarge had no problems taking care of the arrangements. Once more, he had donned his favorite style of clothing, which was the wrong thing to do. He was stopped by a city policeman as he left a club known as a rendezvous point for unsavory characters and questioned at some length. His passport and some fast talking turned him loose. It gave him a scare. If he'd been fingerprinted he'd have been caught, and he knew it. He changed to more conservative dress.

Before leaving Buenos Aires, LaFarge and Sèvres had agreed that when LaFarge finished his business in the United States it would be better if, instead of returning, he set up shop in Mexico City.

After Chicago, he had to make one stop in Minneapolis. It was in that city that his recklessness proved expensive. Somewhere along the line, LaFarge had received information that his partner, Sèvres, had been arrested in Buenos Aires. The news that the narcotics ring had been destroyed inspired LaFarge to make some deals of his own. He thought, and correctly so, that the Minneapolis people didn't know about the arrests in Argentina. He accepted a lot of cash for merchandise he knew he couldn't deliver.

Word came to Minneapolis about Sèvres before LaFarge had time to leave. The people there decided to handle things their own way. An attempt was made to shoot LaFarge in his hotel room. He escaped, but the short if inconclusive gun battle attracted the police. One of his assailants wasn't as lucky. When brought in to the police station he told all he knew. Now LaFarge was wanted in the United States for dealing in narcotics.

If LaFarge knew this, it would have had to be by accident. His subsequent actions tend to show that he did not. He arrived in Mexico City under the name of Villemain, entering the country on Thursday, October 3.

He now adopted another name, Jacques Imbert. There were too many people who might be looking for Henri Villemain. Soon, disgarding any caution, he began operating in his Paris style. The black suits and yellow shirts came back.

He became acquainted with the underworld types in the city and started a pimping operation. His native skills rapidly asserted themselves. He took over three call girls from another pimp and recruited four more girls.

The Mexico City Police became aware of him and his activities. Evidently LaFarge realized this because almost at once he dropped out of sight. His business was continued by one of his lieutenants, a Mexican national named Luis Valdez.

Valdez was a small-time crook, better known by the police for his association with racketeers than for anything he had done himself. He thought LaFarge was the greatest thing he'd seen since Humphrey Bogart in the role of Mad Dog Earl. He emulated LaFarge's clothes, manner, and narrowed eyes. The police arrested him on an assault charge the evening of November 18.

LaFarge didn't wait to find out if Valdez could keep his mouth shut. He left Mexico, landing at El Paso International Airport, on November 19. He had made a wise choice. Valdez couldn't stop talking. If he had had any idea how close the police were to finding him, LaFarge might have chosen another continent.

·

After the arrest of Paul Sèvres in Buenos Aires, along with other members in his group, word got out that LaFarge was part of the operation.

The National Central Bureau in Argentina sent this information to the General Secretariat in St. Cloud. The National Central Bureau in the United States was now contacted and told that LaFarge was probably traveling in America. Even though an intensive search was made, it was not until the Minneapolis Police arrested one of the men trying to shoot LaFarge that LaFarge's alias was known.

The Interpol red notice now contained not only the known aliases and murder warrant from France but also a United States warrant on narcotics charges, a warrant from Argentina on narcotics charges, and a warrant from Mexico for violation of prostitution laws.

With the arrest of Valdez in Mexico City, LaFarge had run

out of trouble-free aliases. El Paso could not supply him with any contacts for false identification. LaFarge had no connections in the border city. It was the idea of finding a place where he wasn't known that had prompted him to choose El Paso.

He intended to stay for a while, close enough to Mexico so he could easily go there if he chose while at the same time keeping an international border between himself and the Mexico City Police. He had no inkling that the National Central Bureaus of the two countries were coordinating efforts to track him down.

If he had tried to cross the border at this time, he would have been caught at once. His photograph and fingerprints were at every U.S. and Mexican border city.

And then, at about nine in the evening on December 6 in the dining room of the Howard Johnson Motor Lodge on Interstate Highway 10, LaFarge's luck went sour.

He was sitting at a table discussing possible narcotic deals with a Mexican national, a small-time racketeer named Jose Herrera. The two spoke in low voices, quickly and in Spanish. From time to time they looked at the people seated around them to see if anyone was interested in their talk. They didn't look closely enough.

In the nearest booth to their table, an off-duty city detective, Nick Kellog, had been eating a hamburger and listening to their conversation. Fluent in Spanish he hadn't missed much, and he had heard enough to decide to do some follow-up work.

When LaFarge left the restaurant and went to his rented car, Kellog took down the license number and got in touch with the police. The police discovered the car had been rented to one Jacques Imbert. It was action time.

The address on the rental contract was local—a motel with separate cabins for its guests. Imbert was paying rent by the week on cabin number 10, located behind the motel office.

As LaFarge was such a hot police item under his own name or any of his aliases on record with Interpol, the cabin was approached carefully and by many armed policemen.

Detectives Jason and Stockdale, holding revolvers, moved to the cabin door. Next to the cabin, crouching by the rented car, two men covered the door with rifles.

The motel cabins were not new. One quick solid kick by Stockdale broke the door lock and slammed the door open, banging it heavily against the inside wall.

LaFarge was completely surprised as the two detectives leaped into the room pointing their guns at him. He was lying on his bed in his shorts and socks. Although his revolver was on the night table within easy reach, he made no move for it. Without a struggle, LaFarge was handcuffed and taken into custody.

And now came a strange turn of events. While LaFarge was held in El Paso and the information about his arrest was sent to the interested authorities, a dispute arose as to which country had first rights to him.

Extradition requests were made by France, Argentina, and Mexico. Minnesota wanted him for violation of state narcotics laws, and the United States federal government also wanted him.

The extradition race was won by Minnesota. They flew two men down to escort LaFarge back for trial. The reason given for surrendering LaFarge to Minnesota was that they were the first ones to finish the paperwork. France, Argentina, and Mexico had to submit their requests through diplomatic channels. It took more time. The federal government was content to slap a detainer on LaFarge to have its chance at him when Minnesota was finished.

LaFarge was tried and convicted in early 1975 by Minnesota. France, which wants him on a murder charge, has a hold on him, as do Mexico and Argentina. They'll have to wait a long time. Léon LaFarge was sentenced to twenty years' imprisonment in the Minnesota State Penitentiary.

Chapter 11

Léon LaFarge, ruthless and a cop killer, is the type of seasoned criminal who is capable of anything. Interpol and various police forces have dealt with this kind for many years. They know what to expect. Sometimes, however, they get surprised by the same ruthless traits when exhibited by a teenage criminal. Especially when that criminal is a girl.

•

In Quebec City, Quebec, Canada, on the morning of November 10, 1974, a Sunday, two people stood in front of a minister to be joined in marriage. Not many attended the wedding. There were perhaps ten or eleven seated in the church when the ceremony began.

The bride, Cora Linnet, was tall and slender with long blond hair that hung straight down her back. The minister had noticed a slight cast in her left eye but didn't think it made her less attractive. He thought she was a very pretty girl.

The groom, Richard Blackman, age thirty-seven, was nineteen years older than his bride. He was also a half inch or so shorter. He had black hair and brown eyes and was a convicted murderer serving a life sentence in a Quebec prison.

He had been given a three-day liberty from prison to marry Cora Linnet under a special program initiated by the prison warden. This Sunday was the first of the three days. He was due back behind the walls on the night of November 12, no later than nine o'clock.

During his seven years in prison, Blackman had become a trusty and was considered a model prisoner. Before his murder conviction, he'd been a bookkeeper and had never broken the law. On the day he decided to steal from the company safe, he had been caught in the act by his assistant. He had panicked, picked up a long sharp letter opener, and stabbed her. She died the same day. It was the only act of violence Blackman had ever committed.

Cora Linnet was eleven years old when Blackman was convicted. She was thirteen when she began to write to him. It was a classroom project. She was the only one in the class to choose a prison inmate for a pen pal.

Blackman, who was unmarried, mild, and shy, welcomed the correspondence with the schoolgirl. Over the years the letters progressed from the stiffly curious to warm and friendly and then to love. After Cora had turned seventeen, she wrote to Blackman that she wanted to marry him.

He was against it, for many reasons, including of course his address. What good would it do to get married? It was senseless. Cora persisted, however, and he had finally agreed. He had every intention of returning after the three days. The prison authorities knew this. They knew Blackman. Unfortunately, they didn't know Cora.

The couple had picked this day because it was the Sunday following Cora's eighteenth birthday. She lived alone with her mother, and her mother had refused to give permission for Cora to marry a prison inmate. Now that Cora was old enough to get married without consent, the wedding could take place.

Cora had dropped out of high school in her junior year to work in a supermarket. Her mother received little income, so the extra money Cora brought home might have had something to do with the mother's withholding permission.

The few friends who had gone to school with Cora thought she was a bit odd. She brooded a lot, they said, and also never dated. All she would talk about was her man in prison. Although Cora refused dates, she was not sexually inexperienced. Before he had walked out, her father had raped her several times. She had been twelve then. Three years later, she and her mother got word that the father had been killed in an automobile accident in the United States.

When the short wedding ceremony was over, Cora kissed her new husband and led him from the church to a rented car. They were planning to spend their three days at a motel on the outskirts of the city. At least that's what Richard Blackman thought. Cora had other plans.

While she drove to the motel, she explained that she had a few surprises for him in the motel room. One of them was a suit of new clothes. She didn't want him to have to wear the clothes provided for the occasion by the prison. Once inside the room, after she had closed and locked the door, she announced that he would never again go behind bars.

Blackman tried to make her understand that he had no choice. It was a special privilege to be given three days. If he failed to return, it might destroy the program for the other inmates.

Cora brushed aside his arguments. She didn't care about the others. She was only interested in him. And, she made clear, her mind was made up. He was not going back.

Blackman showed her the practical side.They had no safe place to hide. They would spend their lives running. Eventually, he was sure, he would be caught and would lose any chance of parole. And another thing, they had no money.

She laughed at his words. It was easy to get money. They would steal it. She was shocked that he hadn't thought of it himself. No, money was not going to be a problem. And as far as the police finding them was concerned, they wouldn't be around to be found.

She then produced the surprises she had promised. First came the new suit from the closet. Then, from her purse, she held up two passports and two plane tickets. She was trembling with excitement. "They'll never find you under a new name and in another country."

She moved to a suitcase and opened it. "Look at this." She reached under some clothing, and when her hand came out it held a pistol. "We can get all the money we need with this."

Blackman, torn between his sense of freedom and his duty to return to prison, wavered. He wasn't a real criminal type, he explained. What he had done had been a sudden action he had regretted ever since. He couldn't bring himself to commit crimes to make a living.

"You're making a big mistake," he said. "I can't do what you want. I'd be afraid to try."

She quickly told him not to worry about it. If he was afraid to use a gun, well, she wasn't. Everything would work out all right.

Blackman had to make a decision. It didn't take him long. He had been without a woman for seven long years. He agreed to her ideas.

The next morning the couple left the motel and drove to Montreal. They abandoned the rented car at Dorval International Airport.

They took an Air Canada flight to France, arriving at eight-forty on the morning of November 12, the same day Blackman was due back in the prison. Immigration checked them through under the false passports, which gave their names as Donald and Norma Chaney. They stayed in Paris until Friday, November 15, then took an SAS flight from Le Bourget Airport to Oslo, arriving at about six the same evening.

The short stay in Paris had exhausted most of their funds. They took an airport bus into the center of town and checked into a cheap hotel. That evening and most of the night they planned their next moves.

Blackman was already having second thoughts about things. According to Cora, he would hardly speak, and when she did get him to say something it usually was to say that they had made a terrible mistake.

Cora, on the other hand, was full of ideas. When she had examined all of them, she came back to their first one, which was to use the gun in a robbery. Blackman had forgotten about it.

He wanted to know how she brought it through customs. Did she realize what would have happened if it had been spotted?

"The point is," she said, "that it wasn't spotted." She had kept it in her purse all the way from Canada.

Cora showed him the money they had left. It came to about fifty Canadian dollars in assorted currencies. She went on to explain that by now he was the object of a police search and not having money was the surest way to get caught.

The next day, Saturday the sixteenth, they stepped out of

the hotel only once, to get food. That night, with Cora now completely in charge, they went out to try for some money.

Cora had selected the target, a rooming house catering to students on Josefinesgate. The rooming house, located on the first two floors of a gray building, was in a residential neighborhood of well-cared-for private homes.

The two slipped on stocking masks, then pushed open the door to the manager's office. Both the manager and his wife were there and were shocked to see the pair enter, a gun pointed menacingly.

As usual, Cora was prepared. She had brought tape and rope with her and they tied their victims to chairs and taped their mouths shut. They took fifteen-thousand crowns from the cash box, cut the telephone wire, and left. The robbery had taken less than ten minutes.

Back in their hotel room, neither could sleep. Blackman was too nervous and frightened, Cora too excited. She paced around the room, retelling and reliving the feelings she had during the robbery.

It was at this time that Blackman began to be afraid of her. "I'm not a violent man," he was to say later. "I could see and feel the violence in her and the excitement. It frightened me."

He wasn't wrong about his eighteen-year-old bride. The next night they found another rooming house to rob. Once again, donning the stocking masks, they surprised and tied up the manager and his wife. Cora counted the money in the cash box and said through the mask, "There must be more than this."

She undid the tape covering the woman's mouth. She asked for more money. The woman spoke little English. She made Cora understand, however, that there wasn't any more money. Cora reacted angrily. She slapped the woman across the face, twice.

The manager, securely tied, squirmed in his chair. Cora told Blackman to quiet him down.

"How?" Blackman asked.

"Break his head with that lamp." She pointed to a large table lamp.

Blackman picked up the lamp, jerking it loose from the wall socket. He stood over the bound man and raised the lamp in the air. Finally, he couldn't do it.

Cora, watching him, cursed. She took the lamp from her husband and smashed it down on top of the man's head.

The lamp shattered, spewing shards of glass and porcelain about the room. Blood ran from the man's head. His wife screamed.

Blackman ran for the door, yelling to Cora to follow. Cora was in no hurry. While Blackman stood at the door, Cora put the tape back over the woman's mouth. Then she stepped back one step and smacked the gun barrel into the woman's temple. As the woman sagged forward, Cora hit her again. The second blow was unnecessary. The first had knocked her out.

Now Cora turned to the man. He was struggling against the ropes, blood running into his eyes. Cora reversed the pistol in her hand and using the gun as a hammer drove it into the man's head several times. When she was satisfied he was completely unconscious she walked over to Blackman.

"Now we can go," she said.

"You may have killed him."

"So what?" she replied.

Blackman now wanted to leave Oslo. He explained to his wife that the police would look everywhere for them. They had spoken English in front of this last couple, and it would narrow the search. There were not that many English-speaking tourists in Norway at this time of year.

Cora disagreed, but after Blackman kept insisting she consented to go to Stockholm. He wanted to go still further away. Any Scandinavian country would be risky. Better to try France or Italy.

Cora told him she was running things and she would make the decisions. When Blackman stopped acting like a frightened Boy Scout, she said, then he could be in charge. Meanwhile, they would do what she thought best.

Evidently Cora was waiting for Blackman to play a different role. She must have assumed that his conviction for murder meant he was a pretty tough character. She attributed his present behavior to his nerve's being softened by prison walls and thought it only a matter of time before he would come around.

Blackman had no illusions about his wife. He wasn't sure what to do. He had gone along with the robberies because he didn't feel he had any choice and besides, they did need the money. He didn't want to hurt anyone. Cora, he was to say, had a lust for hurting people. She had glowed when handing out blows with the pistol. He didn't understand it.

By morning, the eighteenth of November, Cora had changed her mind. They would stay in Oslo one more day and after another robbery they would go to Spain. He had been right about getting completely out of the area, she said, but they needed more money. All they had was a lousy three and a half thousand dollars in Norwegian money.

Blackman objected. It was too risky to try the same thing again. The police would be looking for them. They might even be stopped in the street just because they were English-speaking tourists.

She laughed at everything he said, telling him that if he was too scared to do it again, he could wait for her in the hotel and she would get the money herself. At this he agreed to accompany her.

This time the choice for the night's business was a sixty-room pension near the East Railroad Terminal. In front of the office door on the second floor, they put on the stocking masks and Blackman knocked.

The manager, Malle Johans, came to the door with a word of admonition on his lips. Blackman had knocked too loudly for the hour. The noise might disturb the sleeping guests.

Cora shoved the pistol into his face and backed him into the room. When they were all inside, Blackman locked the door.

The manager's wife, Inger, started out of her chair but sank back at the sight of Cora's gun, which was two inches from her husband's face.

Cora demanded money. Malle Johans shrugged. "You

better put the gun away," he said. "We have no money." His English was perfect. It was so good because he had lived fourteen years in Toronto.

Cora motioned him to a chair, and Blackman began to tie Inger to her chair. Malle remained standing.

Cora pointed the gun at his head. "If you don't go sit in that chair, I'll kill you."

He didn't move. She pulled the trigger. The blast of the gun drew a scream from Inger Johans, a yell from Blackman, and a laugh from Cora. The bullet had shattered Malle's jawbone. He put his hands to his face and crumpled to the floor.

Cora giggled and pointed the revolver at Inger. "Where's the money?"

Inger Johans kept her eyes on her husband. He was lying on his stomach, not moving. She couldn't tell if he was alive or not. She continued staring at him, in a state of shock.

Cora walked next to her and put the gun to her temple. "Where's the money?" she asked again.

Blackman yelled out that someone was coming. He ran to his wife, spun her around by the shoulder, and pulled her toward the door.

There was a loud knocking on the door. Inger Johans took the moment to scream a warning. At the same time Malle Johans groaned and tried to roll over.

Cora looked around wildly, yanked herself free of Blackman, and fired twice at the door. Her first shot knocked out the lock while the second blasted through the lower paneling.

There was the sound of feet running away. Whoever had been outside the room was leaving in a hurry.

Blackman kicked open the door, and he and Cora ran down the stairs and into the street. Lights were coming on in the windows of the pension. The noise had awakened most of the guests.

Cora pushed her husband in the direction of the nearest corner, urging him to run. As they raced for the end of the block, Blackman told Cora to throw away the gun. She dropped it into the gutter.

Chapter 12

Tuesday night, November 12, 1974. The air is crisp and cold and promises to become colder still. Nine o'clock has come and gone. At the prison, Richard Blackman is almost an hour overdue.

In the warden's office, the big white-faced clock on the wall says it is ten minutes to ten. The warden is at his desk, staring at the clock. Next to him, the lieutenant in charge of the yard, the prison psychologist, and two officers follow his eyes and also stare at the clock.

They have all heard that Blackman and his new wife left the motel. Cora's mother could supply no information as to where they might have gone.

It is the first time since the special-privilege program started that an inmate has failed to return on time. Blackman had also been guilty of not letting them know where he was at all times. No decision has been made about the penalty for that. The big concern is whether Blackman will return.

Cigarettes are passed around. The warden and one of the guards light up. No one wants to say the obvious. They are hoping there has been some delay in Blackman's return that can be explained. They know, deep down, that there has not been. The warden stubs out his cigarette and tells the group they will consider Blackman an escapee at midnight.

There are two or three small conversations while the hands of the clock move inevitably toward twelve. The talk is about nothing significant. It dies quickly. The large hand comes up over the small, covering it.

The warden picks up the phone and dials the Quebec City Police. He requests a pickup on Richard Blackman. He reads the statistical information on his inmate from a prison record file. Height, weight, color hair, color eyes, identifying marks, last known address (the motel) flow into the phone in a steady stream.

The Quebec City Police want a national alert. After all, the man is a convicted murderer.

The warden doesn't want that. The resulting publicity will damage the program for other inmates. He explains that Blackman is not a violent type. He will probably be holed up with his wife somewhere, trying to get in some more time with her. It isn't necessary to make a national case out of it.

He replaces the receiver and tells his group the police don't agree. It will be a national hunt. He suggests that they should go to sleep. He and the lieutenant will stay in the office a little longer, just in case. There is a chance that Blackman may be on his way back right now. There is no conviction in the warden's tone.

•

Quebec City has a population of nearly two hundred thousand people. It has one of the busiest harbors in Canada and is the oldest walled city in North America. This is where the search for Blackman and his bride started. Cora is now an accessory to his escape and is wanted as well.

On November 15, Friday, the Quebec City Police decide Blackman is not in the city. They have tried to help the warden by keeping the hunt local. Now they must make the manhunt national.

The Royal Canadian Mounted Police are asked to help. A nationwide alert is activated on Saturday the sixteenth. On Monday the eighteenth, the National Central Bureau contacts Interpol headquarters in France. A request is made for an international pursuit.

•

In Oslo, although it is a Sunday, November 17, the Oslo Police begin to look for a man and a woman, names unknown and English-speaking. These two have committed an armed robbery in a pension and stolen fifteen thousand crowns. It is thought that the pair is American, Canadian, or possibly British.

During the morning hours of the following night, there is a

report of another armed robbery. It appears to be the work of the same couple. This time, however, two persons have been severely hurt. The man is in the hospital with a concussion and fractured skull, the woman with a broken cheekbone. They have both been pistol-whipped by the female assailant. The theft amounted to five thousand crowns. Both victims are certain the robbers were Americans.

The laborious routine of checking all tourist accommodations to find a couple matching the descriptions given by the victims is started as part of the police investigation.

Two couples are picked up and brought in to police headquarters for questioning. One is a husband-wife team of travel writers. They establish their identities and profession and whereabouts on the night in question. They are released within the hour. The other couple is questioned for a longer time. Finally, they are able to prove they were at a party with some local Oslo people.

As the day turns into night, the police become anxious. Men are posted at the airport, bus depots, and railroad. All they really know about the hunted couple is that the woman is blond and a little taller than the man.

Just before midnight, on Monday, the police are called to the scene of an attempted armed robbery. Again, a pension has been the target. A man has been shot in the face. The man's wife is almost hysterical. The description given by the wife and the description by several roomers who watched the assailants run down the street convince the police it is the same couple they want for the other two robberies.

Inger Johans also gives the police an important clue. The couple is Canadian. She can tell the difference between an American and a Canadian accent.

The other witnesses tell the police the robbery took place less than thirty minutes ago. While the police continue to question people, an amublance comes to take Malle Johans to the hospital. He has lost a lot of blood, but he is not in serious danger.

The Oslo Police spread out over the city, on foot, in cars.

There are not many people on the streets at this hour. They feel they have a good chance of catching the couple if they haven't already ducked into some shelter.

.

Blackman wanted to find a taxi. He thought it would get them off the street and into their hotel room before any police arrived at the pension. He felt it was too risky to be out on the streets.

"Waving down a taxi is more risky," Cora said. It would expose them to any passing police cars. And there was also the chance the taxi driver would remember them and where he had taken them. No, it was better to make their way back on foot, sticking to the shadows of buildings.

"We have to leave Oslo," Blackman said. There was a morning train going to Stockholm that would leave at about six-thirty. Because of the stocking masks no one knew what they looked like, and if they got out quickly they would probably make it.

Cora talked about stealing a car but Blackman dissuaded her. Unless the keys were in the car, he would not know how to start it. She accepted his argument.

They got back inside the hotel without being seen. Neither could sleep. Cora began to get angry with her husband because he had made her throw the gun away. Once she even said something about going back to get it.

They packed their few belongings, Cora carrying all the money in her purse, and got to the station in time to board the train just before it left. Cora wore flat shoes and slumped as she walked. She had thought the police would probably know about the difference in height between her husband and herself.

Although there were men posted in the railroad station, somehow they did not think to stop the couple. Probably it was because Cora and Blackman separated before entering the station and got on the train in different cars.

Once seated in a second-class section, Cora told Blackman that their troubles were over. Even though they didn't have the gun, she said, they would be able to get one in Stockholm. After that he might even get his nerve back, she hoped.

•

A red notice was sent out from the General Secretariat to all the member nations. Interpol had received the request for aid on the eighteenth and had sent the notice the morning of the twentieth, a Wednesday.

In Ottawa, the National Central Bureau had gotten a photograph of Cora, taken a year earlier. They transmitted this to Interpol Headquarters, and it was relayed to other National Central Bureaus.

In Oslo, the police found the hotel the Blackmans had used the same day the Interpol red notice arrived in Norway. Now they knew whom they were looking for, the false passports notwithstanding. The alias, Chaney, was telexed into Interpol, St. Cloud, to be sent out as additional information to all the Interpol members.

In Stockholm, Wednesday night, November 20, Cora and Blackman left their hotel, the Wasa, and went to a club on Gamla Stan where they spent the evening listening to rock and folk music. They also tried to make some definite plans.

They had an argument. Cora wanted to remain in Stockholm. Blackman wanted to leave as soon as possible. He thought there was a lot of danger in staying. He was certain, he said, that all the Scandinavian countries would be alerted. He suggested that they leave the next morning.

She didn't understand why he was so nervous. The robberies had been in Oslo. They were in Stockholm, a different country. No one wanted them in Sweden. What had they done except act like a couple of tourists?

Blackman didn't see it that way. Didn't she know that some countries have reciprocal agreements about police matters? If Norway wanted them, there was a good chance the Swedes would help.

Cora scoffed at him. She had put up with his lack of nerve long enough. Evidently his time in prison had sapped his will so thoroughly that he would never get it back. If that were so, why then he could go on his own. She would give him some of the money and he could do whatever he wanted. As for her, she intended to stick around, but not with a weakling.

When they returned to the hotel they had nothing to say to each other. Blackman made one more attempt before they went to bed to get her to see things his way. She refused.

In the morning, now Thursday the twenty-first, Cora gave her husband some money and told him to clear out. Again he tried to change her mind, but she was adamant. He was a failure in her book, and she wasn't interested in him.

Blackman left his clothes in the hotel and went to find out about getting a flight to Italy. He took the airline bus from the air terminal on the Vasagatan to Arlanda Airport.

Ten minutes after he walked into the airport, Richard Blackman was in police custody. The Interpol red notice had done its work. The police in the airport had spotted him almost from the moment he had walked in.

Blackman was not reticent. He detailed his adventures with Cora for the benefit of the investigating detectives. He was locked up and a telex sent to Interpol-Oslo, Interpol-Canada, and the General Secretariat.

·

Cora did not spend much time in the hotel room after her husband left. She went out, taking her purse with her money to find a place to have some breakfast. Her choice was the railroad station cafeteria. There she quickly struck up a conversation with a young English tourist named Martin Freeman.

Freeman was in the middle of a four-month automobile trip through Europe. He had a Volkswagen camper and eagerly decribed its merits to Cora. The best thing about it, he explained, was that he slept in it and didn't have to spend money for rooms.

Cora wanted to know if it wasn't too cold during the night but Freeman said he had an electric heater and was comfortable on the coldest nights. He offered to show her the camper, telling her about all the gadgets he had installed to make it like a home.

At the time they left the cafeteria to look at Freeman's

pride the Stockholm Police were inspecting Cora's hotel room. The police posted a man inside and one in the lobby. They knew she had to return for her clothes.

They were due to be surprised, for Cora had made a quick decision while looking through the camper. Freeman had said he was leaving for Denmark at once and Cora had asked to go with him.

Freeman asked the obvious question about Cora's luggage, but Cora had said she would not need to go back to her hotel. Maybe she sensed that her husband would be caught and could lead the police to her, maybe not. In any case, she and Freeman left Stockholm together. She had offered to pay her share of expenses along the way and that was enough for the Englishman. He wasn't the type to ask a lot of personal questions.

To go to Denmark, they decided to drive to Malmö and take the ferry across to Copenhagen. They were in no hurry. They arrived in Malmö at about noon on Friday.

On their way to the ticket office, Cora asked Freeman to buy her a gun before they left Sweden. She would pay for it, she said, but she did not want to be the one to make the purchase.

Freeman refused and, although startled by the request, did not let Cora know it. He later said he thought it such a strange thing to ask that he began to suspect she might be a little unbalanced. He didn't want to say anything to alarm her. However, he did begin to think about breaking off their short relationship. He decided to wait until they reached Denmark. There was something about her that made him nervous.

He need not have worried. While he purchased the ferry tickets, Cora, who was standing next to him, turned to look at a poster. She looked directly into the eyes of a Swedish police officer, Manne Steffan, who recognized her immediately.

As he moved toward her, she tried to run around him, confirming his suspicions. He stopped her and demanded some identification. When she produced her Norma Chaney passport, he took her into custody.

In February 1975, Richard Blackman was extradited and returned to Canada to prison to continue serving his life sentence. Norway has a hold on him in case he is paroled.

Cora Blackman was extradited to Norway, where she is serving a three-year prison sentence for armed robbery. Canada has a hold on her. Although both Blackmans have indicated they want to be divorced, neither has the money to pay for the proceedings. They will remain married for some time to come.

Chapter **13**

Interpol has recorded many ingenious crimes. Some were so well conceived, so carefully detailed, that it seems almost a miracle that the criminals were caught.

Sweden served as the locale for just this type of adventure, although the criminals involved were not Swedish. They had, in fact, come to Sweden after a long journey and, even then, not directly from their own countries.

•

Bodrum, Turkey, when it was known as Halikarnassos, contained one of the seven wonders of the ancient world, the Mausoleum of Mausolus. Today Bodrum contains mostly tourists. There are only a few ruins left to remind the visitors of Bodrum's past glories.

Its chief attractions now are the clear waters of the Aegean, the hot sun, and the relatively low prices. The big sport is skin diving and it brings many people to the town.

It was not strange, then, that two such tourists should meet in Bodrum and find they had a lot in common. They both spoke English, they both loved skin diving, they both enjoyed being in Turkey, and they both were professional thieves.

Charles Eastman was from Exeter, England. He was well known there to the local constabulary and almost as well known in London by Scotland Yard. There was also a file on him in the General Secretariat, for Eastman had often stepped outside of England to commit some of his crimes. He had spent six of his thirty-two years in various prisons in England and on the Continent.

Arnold Berger was not quite so well known in his home town of Philadelphia. That was probably due to its being a much larger city. He was also on file with Interpol, as he had committed crimes in Mexico, Costa Rica, and Canada. He was three years younger than Eastman but had managed to accumulate as much time behind bars in the United States and Canada.

Eastman had come to Bodrum because he rightly suspected he was under police surveillance in England. He wanted to find a place to relax and plan, as he put it, "a big score, safe and profitable."

Berger was delighted to hear that because he had similar reasons behind his trip to Bodrum. After telling this to Eastman, the two rapidly became fast friends.

Eastman wanted to change his profession. He was a burglar, but the police knew his methods too well. Also, he had his heart set on robbing a bank. He had read that when Willie Sutton was asked why he chose banks to rob, Sutton had replied, "Because that's where the money is." Eastman admired that kind of candor. Moreover, he agreed with the thought.

Berger, whose activities ranged from passing bad checks to an occasional mugging, was also looking for a change of work. He thought Eastman was right. Holding up a bank suited him perfectly. He told this to Eastman.

Neither one of them wanted to do another day's time in a prison. They made up their minds to plan a robbery so well put together that the police would not ever know who had done it.

They agreed that the big problem was not the holdup itself but the escape. Anyone could stick a gun in a teller's face and make off with some money. It was what would happen afterward that created difficulties.

Eastman had given the matter a great deal of thought. He had an idea that if the escape was something different, something out of the ordinary experience of the police, they could be successful. He wanted to use a water route to get away.

Berger got excited with that idea. He agreed. What could be more natural for them? They were both experts in the water. If, somehow, they could make their getaway underwater, it should be foolproof.

The two had come to Bodrum in late June 1974. By July 20, they had had a full month of planning behind them. They had worked out several different routines for the escape and had practiced some of them in the surrounding waters.

There was still one problem to be solved before they could go ahead with the robbery. They had to find a bank near a body of water. Also, the body of water had to be near or inside a large city. It wouldn't be much use to find themselves out in an ocean after the holdup.

Their daily routine never varied. Each morning they would rent a small boat and go out diving. In late afternoon, when they returned, they would spend some time napping and then meet for dinner and drinking and plotting until late in the night.

There was no way they could decide on a definite plan until they could look at the target bank. There were too many variables. They racked their brains trying to remember where they had seen a bank that would prove suitable.

Then a stroke of luck came their way. They met and became friendly with a Swedish tourist from Göteborg. He talked a lot about his hometown and explained about the rivers running through the city.

Berger and Eastman were elated. It sounded like what they were looking for. They decided it was time to move. They did not want to waste any more of their funds in Bodrum. There would be a lot of items to purchase for the bank job and the sooner they started, the better.

On August 6, they took the morning bus up to Izmir. They spent the night there and made airline reservations for Paris with a connection to Stockholm. The Swedish tourist had also told them that Stockholm had a lot of water and that it was composed of islands. They thought they should take a look.

They entered Sweden on August 9, at Arlanda Airport. Almost at once they decided to continue to Göteborg. However, they thought it was a good idea to make some of their necessary purchases in Stockholm.

Before leaving Bodrum, one of their ideas was to enter the bank as a couple. One of them would be dressed as a woman.

Because Berger was a burly six-footer and Eastman was barely five feet six, the woman's role fell to Eastman.

Since they knew their escape would be made by water they were planning to wear wet suits under their clothing. This meant the woman's clothes must be of a type to completely cover Eastman. The only thing they could think of that would do the trick was a pants suit. They found a black one that was long enough to come down over the low-heeled woman's shoes that didn't quite fit Eastman, and they purchased a brown wig.

In their hotel room, at the midtown Continental, Eastman tried on his new finery. They realized they had forgotten something important. Eastman needed some makeup to cover over a rather heavy beard. Even when he was freshly shaved the stubble remained.

They bought some pancake makeup, a bright-red lipstick, mascara, and some red nail polish. Eastman was not happy with the nail polish. He explained that after the hold up, though the mascara and lipstick would come off in the water with a little wiping, the nail polish would remain. Berger insisted the nail polish was necessary while they were in the bank. It was important to convince onlookers that a man and a woman had been the robbers. Reluctantly Eastman agreed to wear the polish.

The last thing they bought before leaving Stockholm was a watertight plastic bag that could be hooked into a belt that Berger would wear around his wet suit. This was to carry the money.

It was now time to move on to Göteborg, by rented car. They checked into Göteborg's Hotel Opalen on August 13, a Tuesday. That same day they found the bank they wanted, a branch of the Skandinaviska Banken, located next to the Savean River.

The river curved gently to join another river, the Gotaalv, about a thousand yards downstream. From the juncture of the two rivers, there was a much wider flow of water.

The next day, the fourteenth, they rented a fourteen-foot motorboat, paying for a month's rental in advance. They also took time to look over the bank. It was more than suitable, they decided. It was perfect.

The bank was not large. It had a long counter with three tellers working behind it and two desks against the wall across from the counter. It wouldn't be hard to keep everyone in the bank under their guns.

They spent the next two days exploring the river and trying to figure out the best way to handle their escape. The more they thought over the situation the more impossible it became. To use the boat properly, so it would not be recognized as the escape vehicle, it had to be waiting somewhere out of sight.

Eastman suggested tying the boat up near the junction of the two rivers. After the robbery, they would swim underwater to it.

Berger wasn't sure about this. If it was far enough away so no one would notice it, that would also mean a long underwater swim. They very well might not find it. He didn't want to take that chance.

There was one certain way to find it, Eastman told Berger. If they rigged an underwater line that reached from the boat to the spot where they entered the water, all they would need to do was follow it while submerged.

This idea needed more exploration. First they would have to know if it was a reasonable distance. They discovered a place to tie up the boat on the bank of the Gotaalv just before that river joined the smaller Savean. The point of land separating the rivers at the junction would keep the boat hidden from anyone on the banks of the Savean. The distance they would need to rig the line was about 1,500 yards.

Using their wet suits and aqualungs, they searched the river bottom and found a place to anchor the wire on the remains of a sunken hull of a rowboat in the Savean across from the bank. The other end of the guide wire was attached to the bottom of their motorboat.

The robbery was planned for Tuesday the twentieth, exactly one week from the date of their arrival in Göteborg.

Monday the nineteenth, they finished all their prepara-

114

tions. They placed a change of clothing aboard the boat. They draped a sailcloth from the small cabin to extend to the rear of the boat so they would be hidden from curious eyes when they climbed aboard. An attaché case was purchased and into it went their passports as well as two plane tickets. They had reservations on SAS Flight 495 to Copenhagen, and from there they would change to SAS Flight 567 to Paris. Their luggage, stripped to essentials, was also on the boat.

Everything was timed. Their plane left at one-ten in the afternoon, the day of the robbery. Once on the boat, they would head up the Gotaalv to the first docking point and then grab a taxi to the airport.

The aqualungs were hidden close to the sunken hull in the Savean River, almost directly across from the bank branch. All they had to do was dive into the water after leaving the bank, make the short swim across the Savean, grab the aqualungs, and follow the line the 1,500 yards underwater to the motorboat.

Eastman's pants suit was altered so he could get out of it quickly. Berger had fixed his own pants so they were held together by one hook. Over the top of his wet suit he would be wearing a lightweight zippered jacket. They had practiced getting out of their clothing. Berger could finish a shade faster, and the last part of his job would be to take off Eastman's wig. The last practice time had shown them they could be stripped down to the wet suits in less than twenty seconds.

At fifteen minutes after ten, Tuesday, August 20, Berger and Eastman entered the bank. Except for two male customers, only the bank employees were inside.

Eastman, wearing his black pants suit and his wig and heavily made up, lurched uncomfortably toward the counter in his ill-fitting shoes. He held a purse close to his stomach.

Berger, his jacket zipped up under his throat to hide the wet suit, kept his hands in the jacket pockets. He walked about one step behind Eastman.

Selma Moberg, a teller, looked up as they approached the counter in front of her. She wanted to laugh at the sight of the strange-looking woman clutching her purse because even the heavy makeup could not hide the dark shadow of a beard underneath. She wanted to say something to the girl next to her but thought she better not because the strange creature was close enough to overhear.

At that moment, Eastman reached into his purse and pulled out a revolver. He pointed it at Selma Moberg and demanded some money.

As Eastman drew his gun, Berger also produced a pistol from his pocket and, turning his back to Eastman, forced the two customers to move between the desks and raise their hands. Eastman, meanwhile, was ordering the other tellers to put money on the counter in front of them.

It was very quiet during the robbery. The two men moved rapidly, coordinating their efforts in scooping up the money and dumping it in the watertight plastic bag, which they had brought along in the purse. When the bag was filled, Eastman threw the purse on the floor. There was no use for it anymore.

Holding their guns on the group and warning them that they would shoot the first person to show his face through the door after they left, they backed out of the bank.

Now, the escape phase of the plan took over. As soon as the doors closed, Berger and Eastman ran toward the riverbank. Eastman kicked off his shoes as passersby started to look and point at the odd pair running to the water.

At the entry point, the clothes came off. As Berger ripped off Eastman's wig, Eastman fastened the money bag to Berger's belt. Although they were ready for the water in no longer time than their practice sessions, there was still time for curious people to begin forming a small group around them.

They dove into the water, swimming hard for the hidden aqualungs. At the same moment the people from the bank burst through the doors screaming there had been a holdup. It's doubtful if either Berger or Eastman could hear them.

Everything seemed to be working just as they planned. They found the aqualungs and got them in place and began to make their way along the wire.

Eastman led the way, his feet inches ahead of Berger. The method they had devised for their underwater trip was to keep one hand on the wire and to keep eye contact with each other. It slowed them down but as no one could see them, it didn't make much difference. The most dangerous part of the robbery was behind them.

The guns they had used were resting on the bottom of the river. As they moved along, Eastman wiped the makeup from his face, using his free hand. He had a little trouble seeing. They had made a decision earlier that it was more important to get rid of the makeup than to wear face masks. Because they had the wire guide it was not necessary to see too well.

They passed the junction of the two rivers. Only about five hundred yards more to go. They had marked the spot on the wire with a piece of rope. They were home free now, or so they thought.

Chapter **14**

When Charles Eastman left England to go to Turkey, he thought one of the things he was leaving behind was police surveillance. In fact, he was not. When he took the train from Exeter for London, a routine call let Scotland Yard know that Eastman was out of the Exeter police district. Because of Eastman's long police record, because he was a confirmed repeater of crimes, and because he had no visible means of support, Scotland Yard was interested in keeping an eye on him.

When he took a plane out of the country his destination was known. Scotland Yard informed the General Secretariat, and Interpol at once issued a green notice of warning giving Eastman's photo, fingerprints, arrest record, and other pertinent data to all the National Central Bureaus of the member nations. An addition to the notice stated that Eastman was heading for Turkey.

Turkish immigration confirmed Eastman's entry into their country on June 16. The information was passed on to the General Secretariat.

While in Istanbul, Eastman stayed at the Pera Palace Hotel. He did not stay long, according to the police report. He left for Bodrum by bus on the eighteenth of June, checking out of the hotel that morning. Istanbul Police notified the police in Bodrum and requested a sharp watch on the Englishman.

Arnold Berger was not observed when he left Philadelphia to go to New York to catch his flight to Turkey. Not long afterward, however, the Philadelphia Police, aware that he had slipped out from under their surveillance, made some inquiries. They learned Berger had gone to New York, in all probability with intent to leave the country. They contacted the National Central Bureau in Washington, the Treasury

Department. The Treasury Department informed the General Secretariat, and now a green notice was sent out on Arnold Berger.

Istanbul turned up Berger's entry into their country during a routine check of immigration cards. He had come in a day after Eastman and, it was later learned, he'd also taken a bus to Bodrum.

Soon after Berger's arrival in Bodrum, his quick friendship with Eastman aroused the curiosity of the Bodrum Police. They requested their own National Central Bureau for information on Berger and, of course, received the reply that he, too, was the subject of a green notice.

The Bodrum Police decided that they ought to take some sort of action against the pair. They did not want known criminals mingling with the other tourists. But at the last minute they concluded that Eastman and Berger had met by accident and contented themselves with keeping a close watch on the two.

At no time during their stay in Turkey did Berger or Eastman realize they were being watched. They were shocked when they later found out there was a file covering all their movements in Turkey.

In August, when they left Turkey to go to Sweden, this information was forwarded to the General Secretariat and, through close police cooperation, the Swedish police in Stockholm were able to have a man posted in Arlanda Airport when they arrived. His assignment was to keep tabs on them and see that their actions were continually known to the police. He followed them to the Continental, later checking to be certain they had actually taken a room there.

Interpol-Sweden is the Interpol Sektionen, Rikspolis-styrelsen, located in Stockholm. They sent a message to the General Secretariat confirming that Berger and Eastman were in Stockholm and under observation.

The would-be bank robbers, meanwhile, went about town making their purchases. The police made certain they were not changing their address. The hotel was instructed to notify them in the event their two guests checked out. It was the feeling of the Swedish National Central Bureau that Berger and Eastman were preparing to commit a crime soon. They could not believe the two had come all the way from Bodrum just to see the sights.

On August 13, the Tuesday on which the pair left for Göteborg, the hotel duly notified the police. They had no idea where the two men had gone. No forwarding address had been given.

The next step was to check all the airlines to see if the two had booked a flight either out of or within the country. The airlines could give no helpful information.

There were several possibilities open. The pair might still be in Stockholm but in a different hotel. As hotel registrations are routinely sent in to the police they would know sooner or later, but they did not want to wait that long. The painful task of checking each hotel was begun at once. Another possibility was that they had left the city by train or car. This thinking brought on a check of car rental agencies. It turned up the information that Berger and Eastman had rented a car from Hertz for a two-week period for a "driving trip" through Sweden.

The police now notified every police district in Sweden to be on the lookout for the pair. Their descriptions and the license number of the rented car were included in the messages. Unless Eastman and Berger garaged the vehicle, it would certainly be spotted quickly.

Police all over Sweden began to pay close attention to guest registrations. To keep out of sight it was going to be necessary for Berger and Eastman to hide not only the car but themselves as well.

It did take some time, however, to make these arrangements and notifications. The delay enabled the two men to remain unobserved until August 18, two days before the scheduled robbery.

They were found through the normal hotel registration check. By this time they had solved their escape plan problems, rented the motorboat, set up the guide wire, and made their practice swims.

The only thing the Göteborg Police knew was that they were in the Hotel Opalen. Because they had not made any overt moves to cover their tracks, the police believed that whatever they were planning was not going to be done in Göteborg. Still, they decided to check with the hotel twice each day to make sure they knew where the two were. It was thought unnecesary to put a tail on them.

The man placed in charge of keeping tabs on Eastman and Berger was Detective-Inspector Carl Backman. A fifteen-year veteran of the police force, Backman made it his business to spend an hour watching them on the afternoon of Monday, August 19.

So it happened that he saw them climbing about on the rented boat, putting the sailcloth covering in place. Backman checked out the boat and discovered it had been rented for a full month by the two men. He decided they had something in mind that required the use of the boat, but just what was anyone's guess.

Because Eastman and Berger had no prior bank robberies or armed robberies in their arrest records, they were not suspected of such a plan. Police have found it is rare for a check passer or a burglar to turn to armed robbery, and there was not any reason to think this pair would prove exceptions. It was thought, rather, that they might be planning a large burglary and would hide the loot in the boat.

Another piece of information turned up that afternoon. Police checking the airport found out that Eastman and Berger had plane reservations for an SAS flight to Paris, with a stopover in Copenhagen to change planes. The flight was to leave the next day, at one-ten in the afternoon.

Detective-Inspector Backman and his men tried to put the puzzle, if indeed there was one, in one piece. Although the two men had a boat with twenty days or so left on the rental time, they were leaving the country the next day. Too much activity not to mean something, Backman decided. It appeared that whatever was going to happen would happen during the coming night. If nothing did happen, then it had to be assumed Berger and Eastman were planning to do something outside Sweden with the idea, perhaps, of returning after the job.

Backman immediately assigned a man to watch the hotel. He also stationed a man near the boat. The surveillance was to continue until the pair checked out of the hotel to go to the airport.

All that evening and through the night, Berger and Eastman remained in their room. They came down to the hotel restaurant for breakfast at eight in the morning, looking like any of the other tourists who were moving into the dining room.

Backman, who had stayed up during the night, was not satisfied. Working on instinct, he decided to post a man at the airport so that, if anything surprising happened, the police could stop the two before they escaped.

Interpol-Stockholm, told the latest news about the pair, contacted Interpol-Denmark and Interpol-Paris, passing on the flight times of the planes. And now, with everything done that could be done, the police waited, alert and posted.

The hotel, like the one in Stockholm, had been told to call the police the moment Eastman and Berger checked out. The police officer posted outside the hotel entrance had seen Eastman and Berger go into the dining room to get their breakfast and phoned in the information. He was sure nothing was going to happen. If they had not tried anything during the night, he hardly thought they would try during the day. He was to stay in position until he saw them leave the hotel.

When a group of tourists came through the hotel doors he looked them over quickly and then turned away. If he had looked a bit more closely he might have noticed a peculiar-looking woman among them. He would have also been able to see that her male escort was Arnold Berger. As it was, they slipped past him, not more than ten feet away.

Berger had come down to the hotel desk fifteen minutes earlier to pay the bill. He informed the clerk that they would be remaining in their room for some time. It was part of the careful planning that had gone into the robbery. The hotel clerk as well as one of the bellboys failed to see Berger and Eastman when they left with the tourist group soon afterward.

The police were told that Berger had paid the bill and also what he had said to the clerk about staying in the room. The police instructed the clerk to call them again when they left with their luggage. They had no way of knowing the luggage was already on the boat.

At seventeen minutes after ten, an automatic alarm went off in police headquarters, signaling a bank robbery. Police raced to the scene. They were told that two men, one disguised as a woman, had held up the bank and then jumped into the Savean River. They had crossed to the other side, then suddenly disappeared under the water.

The police moved to the spot used as the jumping-off place and found the discarded wig and clothing. Witnesses told of seeing two men wearing wet suits under their clothing. They had jumped into the river and disappeared after swimming across. No one had seen them surface, not even those curious onlookers who had run along the edge of the river hoping to see when and where they would come up. It was a real mystery and a large crowd had gathered to hear all about it.

•

While the police were asking questions and getting less than satisfactory answers, Eastman and Berger arrived at the boat. As planned, they dumped the aqualungs into the water, then climbed aboard.

Hidden by the sailcloth, they struggled out of their wet suits, hardly drying themselves in their haste to get into their other clothing. As soon as they were dressed, Berger started the motor and Eastman cast off.

•

Police Officer Lagerlof, who had been watching the boat since early in the morning, was startled to see it suddenly rocking in the water. He had seen no one board it and from his vantage point it was impossible for him not to see anyone who tried. He decided it must be rocking from a current or from the wake of a passing boat. He continued watching the boat rock until he realized there was no passing boat nor any current. At the same moment, he saw Eastman lean out over the stern to cast off and heard the motor roar to life.

"Hey," he called out. He was too far away for the men on board to hear him. He was not certain who was on the boat. He had caught only a quick glimpse of Eastman and had not known positively that it was indeed Eastman he was looking at. He rushed to get the information to Backman.

The police investigating the bank robbery had still made no connection between the armed robbers and Eastman and Berger. But there was one person who did make the connection—Detective-Inspector Backman. After receiving the news that the boat was underway, everything had dropped into place for him. The boat, the air reservations, the reports of diving in Bodrum—it all made sense now. He moved quickly.

More men were sent to the airport. Because the police were not certain how and where Berger and Eastman would leave the boat, it was thought best to let them make their unsuspecting way to the Airport. They knew the pair would have to check in at the SAS window before boarding their flight. The police would be waiting for them when they got there.

•

Eastman and Berger walked confidently to the SAS check-in window in the airport terminal building. There was still some nail polish, chipped but visible, on Eastman's fingers. They took their places at the end of the small line at the window and did not seem surprised when two men quickly moved into line behind them, then moved to flank them. The two men looked like anxious businessmen trying to see what was holding up the line.

The police did not know if Berger and Eastman were armed. They did not want any shooting in the airport. As the two men flanked the robbers, two of the men in front of them in the line whipped about and pressed in tightly.

Eastman and Berger were surrounded by four men, two of

124

whom had revolvers pointed at them. They surrendered meekly.

.

Both Arnold Berger and Charles Eastman are now serving long prison sentences in Sweden. Although their plans were well thought out and out of the ordinary, they were trapped finally by a sheet of paper, coded green and also a little out of the ordinary.

Chapter 15

Because police authority is necessarily confined within geographical boundaries, it becomes the job of each nation's National Central Bureau to take up the chase on behalf of the Interpol member that initiated the hunt.

In rare instances, the police from the originating country may travel to another country where they act as advisers to the local National Central Bureau. This occurs in certain high-priority cases when it is believed that combined efforts will produce quicker results. Another determining factor can be the size of a theft. If the sum of money is great enough, the originating nation may feel that travel expenses are justified. One country that had reason to feel that way was Venezuela.

•

In July 1969, a week after Neil Armstrong dazzled the world by placing a foot on the moon, a young couple and their three-year-old daughter walked down an airplane ramp in Caracas, Venezuela. They would eventually lead the police on a nineteen-day, twenty-five-thousand-mile chase.

The couple, Ralph and Mary Edwards, entered Venezuela with United Kingdom passports. Ralph was twenty-six years old, Mary twenty-four. They had come, they said, to build a new life. To go along with this new life, they had adopted new names. They didn't talk about that.

Their passports, as well as their other identity documents, were all under the name Edwards. If Home Office experts in England had seen the passports, they would have been impressed. They were perfectly forged, the work of a very skilled person—Edwards himself. It was just one of his many talents.

There was good reason for the new name. The old one was the subject of a search throughout the United Kingdom and would soon be the focus of an international hunt by Interpol. On his way out of England, Edwards had stopped off in London to hold up a bank. He had taken, at gunpoint, the equivalent of $25,000 in English pounds.

The couple's plan in Caracas was to lead as normal a life as possible. The money would provide the stake to get a good start while Ralph Edwards looked for a job. It would keep the pressure off them so that Mary Edwards could stay at home without worrying and take care of their daughter, Jill.

Within a few days they had found a four-room flat located in a middle-class residential district. After settling in, Edwards began his job hunt.

As the couple's first idea had been to lead an ordinary middle-class life, Edwards decided to become a high school teacher, specializing in English and mathematics. The fact that he had never finished high school himself was no bar to his plan. He had some excellent documents to prove he was actually qualified to teach at the university level. He could also, if needed, produce diplomas showing he was fluent in several languages, not the least of which was Spanish.

He presented these documents, along with his good personality and quick mind, at an interview in a high school close to the district in which he was living.

The school officials were very taken with him and offered him a job teaching English during the coming fall term. The salary wasn't much, but as Edwards had most of the money from his bank holdup hidden in his apartment, he felt it would make a good start. He accepted the position.

When the school term began, he quickly became popular with the students and the other teachers. He was considered a good teacher, helpful, interested in community affairs, and the type who eventually would make a good administrator.

He and his wife lived quietly, entertaining at home and visiting the homes of others. They did not enter into Caracas night life. Everything they did, they did together. It was evident to the community that here was a couple devoted to each other and family life.

By December 1971, Edwards and his wife were thoroughly

sick of their middle-class role. The fact was, quiet living was something that bored them both. They really liked expensive night clubs, good clothes, fancy cars, and all the things money could buy. Edwards decided a job change was in order. He wanted to be near money.

He applied for a position in a bank. The references and credentials he showed during his job interview were outstanding. He could prove, on paper, that he had worked for a year as a loan officer in a large London bank. The references stated that his work was truly superior. He explained his time as a schoolteacher in Caracas as an exploratory thing, to see if he wanted a teaching career. The bankers who interviewed him told him that they were glad he had decided to return to banking. He began the new job January 3, 1972.

The high school was sorry to lose Edwards. They gave him a farewell party and told him they could understand his going to a better opportunity.

The bank work was easy for Edwards. He showed a quick grasp of his duties. It was hard for his fellow employees to believe he had had only one year's experience in a bank.

His superiors found him eager to please, always one of the first workers in when the doors opened in the morning and one of the last to leave at night. They congratulated themselves on their decision to hire him. It was also noticed that whenever Edwards had some free time he used it to help someone else with his work.

As January gave way to February, the city of Caracas prepared for a gigantic festival. It was an event of enough importance to close the schools, banks, shops, and just about everything else for a week's vacation. The festival was to begin the weekend of February 11.

Edwards was especially friendly with two people in the bank, Jose Gomez, the head cashier, and Manuel Diaz, the bank president. One afternoon they asked him if he planned to see the festival during the vacation.

Edwards explained that although he had seen a lot of Europe and a little of the United States, he had seen nothing of South America except the city of Caracas. Because of this, he thought he would use his vacation time to visit Bogotà, the capital of Colombia.

On Friday the eleventh, the bank closed for the festival, not to reopen officially until Monday the twenty-first.

A lot of the people working in the bank left early, at noon and after lunch. The last people in the bank were Edwards and Gomez. Edwards left first, and a little later Gomez left.

When Edwards reached his apartment, his wife and a neighbor greeted him at the door. His wife told him that they were all packed and that the neighbor had agreed to take them to the airport. The neighbor had also offered to keep their daughter while they were away, but the Edwards explained that they always took her wherever they went.

•

During the time the couple was in Caracas, Interpol and its member nations had been looking for Edwards in connection with the London bank robbery. They were having their problems. Nowhere in any police file was there any information, photos, or fingerprints on the wanted man. From descriptions given by bank employees, a police artist had made a likeness that had been identified as that of a man called Miles Taylor. But the police were not able to turn up much on Taylor. He had disappeared. He was supposed to have a wife somewhere but no children. It was sketchy information at best.

Venezuela's National Central Bureau, the Cuerpo Technico de Policia Judicial O.C.N., located in Caracas on Avenida Universidad, had the information about Taylor. That is, they knew he was under suspicion of involvement in a bank robbery. They had no idea that the object of their search frequently walked by their building.

Edwards would have been just as amazed to know his real name was mentioned from time to time behind those doors. He was sure no one was looking for him after all this time. He had said as much to his wife.

On Monday, February 21, the bank where Edwards worked reopened for business. To everyone's surprise, Ralph Edwards was not at his desk on time. It was very busy in the bank, and Edwards was missed. A call was placed to his home, but there was no answer. It was first thought that he had extended his vacation and some eyebrows were raised at the fact that he had neglected to call in.

Jose Gomez, the head cashier, tried to pick up the slack at Edwards' desk. Of course, he found everything in order. Edwards was that type of attentive employee. Then, about an hour after Gomez had begun to work at that desk, he stumbled across something that puzzled him. It was a telex message from a New York bank, confirming the transfer of $426,000 from the Caracas bank.

The two banks did a lot of business together. Part of that business involved transfers of large sums of money. What puzzled Gomez was that the money had been transferred to the account of an R. M. Donald. Gomez knew of no reason why R. M. Donald should have received that sum of money. He did not even know an R. M. Donald. As part of Gomez's job was to keep track of interbank transfers, he thought he had better look into the matter.

His first thought was to call the New York bank, but then he decided to discuss the matter with Diaz, the president. He imagined, at the time, that it was a legitimate transaction, and perhaps Diaz could explain it.

Diaz could not explain anything. After a quick conference they decided to call New York. Gomez did not want to speak with just anyone. If the transfer turned out to be normal, he did not want to spread any rumors in New York. The man he wanted was not coming in for another half hour, he was told. He said he would call back.

A man was sent to Edwards' apartment, meanwhile, to see if he had returned and had not answered the phone because of problems on the line. Strangely enough, Diaz, at this point, simply thought Edwards might be of some help in finding out about the transfer.

The man returned to say that the apartment was still empty. He had talked to a neighbor who said that no one had entered it since Edwards and his family left.

Gomez tried the bank in New York again. This time there

were some results. He learned, for one thing, that the money transferred into the account of R. M. Donald had been withdrawn. At least most of it had. Six thousand dollars remained.

Gomez asked for more information about R. M. Donald. The New York bank said they would check and call back. Gomez and Diaz waited in Diaz's office with deepening suspicions. They continued calling Edwards' apartment, although by now they were almost certain they would get no response. They were right.

New York called back. R. M. Donald could not be reached at the address given on his account card. The reason he could not be reached was that he evidently did not live there. New York had been thorough. They had contacted the firm managing the apartment house and asked about R. M. Donald. The firm had never heard of him. If he was at that address it was not under the name of Donald. There was one more thing. R. M. Donald was not a he, the bank said. It was a woman.

Caracas asked if anyone in the New York bank knew what she looked like. New York asked them to hold the line. They would check with their people.

In a few minutes they were able to give Caracas an answer. R. M. Donald was a young woman, well dressed, wore her hair to her shoulders, a blonde. Oh, yes, there was something else. The day she had withdrawn the money she had a small girl with her, probably her daughter. The girl was, the bank thought, about six or seven years old at the most, maybe younger.

Edwards' wife was well known to Gomez. She did not have long blond hair. Her hair was short and dark. But the child would fit, within a year or two, the age of Jill. It didn't take long before someone mentioned wigs.

There was another conference, this time including a few more bank executives. The information from New York was given out and opinions asked. A quick question was raised. How did Edwards or his wife manage to open the account in New York? Neither one had been out of the country.

"Not that we know of," Gomez put in. "She could have

gone anytime. Edwards obviously wouldn't have mentioned it."

A lot of heads nodded in agreement. An air of finality settled over the meeting. Every head swung around toward Diaz.

The bank president got to his feet. "I think," he said, "we should call the police."

Chapter 16

The Caracas Police moved rapidly. That afternoon they searched Edwards' apartment. They found some clothing and household goods. It seemed normal enough to believe the family might have plans to return.

However, a check with the airlines showed that Edwards had made a large payment for overweight luggage. It didn't seem likely that for a short vacation to Bogotà he would take that much.

Information from Venezuelan immigration stated that the family had not come back into the country at any port of entry. Venezuelan immigration also told the police that their records showed Mary Edwards had left and returned to the country two times during January and February. Both times her destination had been New York City.

The next day, Tuesday, February 22, a national alert for the couple was broadcast throughout Venezuela. This was done in case Edwards tried to slip back into the country illegally. The next step was to get in touch with the National Central Bureau in Caracas.

Interpol-Venezuela initiated a ten-nation alert and forwarded the available information on Edwards to the General Secretariat in St. Cloud. All of this was routine procedure. They then did something not at all routine. They decided to chase Edwards with their own men. Two detectives were picked from the staff of the Venezuelan National Central Bureau. One, Vincente Ramos, was a ten-year police veteran specializing in cases of embezzlement and fraud. The other was thirty-year-old Carlos Vargas, whose specialty was foreign languages and forgeries.

Ramos and Vargas flew to Bogotà on Wednesday the twenty-third. Their instructions were to work with the police of the Colombian National Central Bureau. They brought along an artist's drawing of Edwards and his wife as well as other descriptive information supplied to them by bank employees.

In Bogotà, Ramos and Vargas were met by police from Interpol-Colombia. They were also given some information. The Edwards family had taken a morning Avianca flight to New York the day before, Tuesday. United States immigration had confirmed their entry.

The two Venezuelans checked with their office in Caracas. The orders were definite. They were to follow and aid in the identification and arrest of Edwards. They left for New York the next morning.

An officer from Interpol-U.S.A. met them at Kennedy International Airport. The plan was to check the New York area for Edwards, a tedious and difficult task. They would get help from the New York City Police. At the same time, all airlines were asked to keep an eye on passenger reservations. If Edwards or his wife booked a flight, the airlines were to notify the police.

Friday morning, Japan Air Lines informed the police that Ralph and Mary Edwards and their daughter had taken a JAL flight to Tokyo on Thursday, the same day Ramos and Vargas had come into the United States. The police officers had landed in the evening, the Edwardses had left in early afternoon.

A call was placed from Interpol-U.S.A. to Interpol-Japan in Tokyo asking that the Japanese Police try to locate the couple. The General Secretariat issued circulars to every member nation.

Ramos and Vargas, beginning to feel tired now from plane travel, reached Tokyo's Haneda International Airport at six-thirty on the morning of February 27. The chase had moved into its fifth day. The two detectives had already covered ten thousand miles.

Japanese immigration was able to confirm the arrival of the Edwards family. A check of the airlines showed that they had not left Japan by air. Further checking showed they had not left by ship. They had to be somewhere in Japan. Tokyo, most probably, said the Japanese Police. It would take some time, but sooner or later they would be found. As Caucasians they could hardly melt into the crowds.

Orders were issued that all reservations lists for air travel be checked daily. Late in the evening of the twenty-ninth, Tuesday, a familiar name turned up on one of the lists. The name was Miles Taylor. Traveling with him were Naomi and Ann Taylor, his wife and daughter. The name triggered the memories of the Interpol people. This Miles Taylor might well be the man wanted by the police in London for a 1969 bank robbery. There was a very good chance, the police concluded, that Taylor and Edwards were the same person.

The General Secretariat was fed the information and also the news that the Edwardses or Taylors had left Japan for Hong Kong. Once more they had slipped past the police alert.

Vargas and Ramos continued the chase. They landed at Kaitak International Airport in Hong Kong in the afternoon on Wednesday, March 1.

Interpol-Hong Kong at once began to check the hotels. The name Miles Taylor was listed with airlines, travel agents, and banks, in case Taylor tried to change some money.

•

In the Hotel Plaza on Gloucester Road, in a suite on the twentieth floor, Ralph Edwards and his wife were preparing to move on to another city. Ironically, they were registered in the hotel under the name of Edwards, while the police were searching for Miles Taylor. Ralph and Mary Edwards had no idea how close the police were to them. But they had reservations on Cathay-Pacific Airlines for a morning flight to Manila.

Mary wanted to rest. She told Edwards that she was exhausted, and also she wanted to see Hong Kong. She might not get another chance.

Edwards told her he was tired too. But they had to keep moving. It was all part of his plan to confuse the police. After all, he told her, hadn't everything gone just the way he had said it would? Soon all the traveling would come to an end, but now they had to put up with it.

The next morning, without encountering any problems, they boarded their plane and flew to Manila. The date was March 3.

•

Ramos and Vargas found out about the Manila flight the next day. The name Edwards had been added to the Hong Kong alert, but the thought had come too late. The Venezuelans followed to Manila, arriving two days after the Edwardses, on a Sunday. It was the twelfth day of the chase, and the detectives had close to thirteen thousand miles in air travel.

Interpol-Manila had been alerted and had tried to locate the Edwardses. They had done a thorough job, they explained to Vargas and Ramos. If the Edwardses hadn't slipped out of the country they would have to be somewhere other than Manila. They were not in the city, the police were certain.

"Then where could they possibly have gone?" Vargas asked.

"To an outlying area," was the reply.

There are eleven main islands in the Philippines. The couple might have been on any one of them. It would take a long time to find them.

The Manila-Interpol people had a welcome surprise for them. "Would the two police officers mind riding in a helicopter?"

All day Monday, using helicopters, the Manila Police and the Venezuelans went from island to island. They found no trace of Edwards. On their weary return, they received word that the fugitives might be in the city of Iloilo, on the island of Panay. Some Americans or English people had recently arrived there by boat.

The next morning the helicopters took off for Panay. With the help of the local police, the visitors discovered that a family had come to Iloilo, a family of six Canadians. In a discouraged mood, the hunters returned to Manila.

136

They were even more discouraged and angry that night when they learned that a Miles Taylor and family had taken a Malaysian Airlines flight to Kuala Lumpur while they had been in Panay.

"Why hadn't the airlines told the police about the Taylors taking tickets to Malaysia?" Ramos demanded.

"Because we were keeping our eyes open for Edwards. The name Taylor didn't register until later."

Ramos and Vargas arrived at Kuala Lumpur International Airport on Wednesday, March 8, exhausted. They could not understand how Edwards, along with a wife and child, could possibly continue. If they, two police officers, were dragging so, just what condition were the Taylors, or Edwardses, in?

Malaysia seemed to be a dead end. The police had looked through the immigration cards but had found neither Edwards nor Taylor.

"If they were one step ahead of us they might have used another identity," Ramos said. "See if there was a family of three on that flight."

After looking over the passenger manifest the police assured Ramos that no family of three had been on the flight and that it was evident a mistake had been made.

Now Ramos called Manila. He asked for a recheck of the information that had said the Edwardses took a flight to Malaysia. The answer came with a strong apology. There had been a mistake in Manila. The Edwardses had actually flown to Singapore.

A quick check with Singapore confirmed the fact. It also gave Ramos and Vargas the information that Edwards had flown from Singapore to Bangkok.

"Are you positive?" Ramos wanted to know.

They were told the information was valid. "You can always check with immigration in Thailand," Singapore suggested.

This was done, using the network between the National Central Bureaus of Malaysia and Thailand. The news reached Kuala Lumpur that Ralph, Mary, and Jill Edwards were in Bangkok. The police had them under surveillance. They would keep watch on them until Ramos and Vargas arrived.

Not surprisingly, the two Venezuelans were not overly excited. They had been too close before without results.

In the morning, they took a Thai International plane to Bangkok. Police from Interpol-Thailand met them at the airport. It was March 10, Friday.

Vargas told Ramos later that when the police greeted them he fully expected to be told that the Edwards family had slipped away again. Instead, the police asked if they wanted to leave their luggage at the airport and go at once to the hotel to confront Edwards. He was still there.

•

In a luxury hotel on Patpong Road, the Edwardses were relaxing. Jill, who had shown the least effects of the travel, was fast asleep in a connecting room. Ralph was lying on the bed, dressed but with his shoes off. He had a drink in his hand although it was only the middle of the morning. Mary was having plain fruit juice. She asked Ralph if he thought it a good idea to be drinking scotch so early in the day.

He told her that it was time to relax a little. They had just one more long trip to make to end their travels. That trip would be to Argentina. He was certain that if the police had managed to trail them at all, they would think that he was settling somewhere in the Far East. Instead, he planned to double back to South America.

"Once we reach Argentina," he said, "we'll live like kings."

Mary Edwards was to remember the way her husband looked at the moment he said this to her. It stuck in her mind because of something else that happened that very instant. There was a loud knocking on their door and some muffled words about the police.

Edwards swung himself off the bed and stood up. "Don't open that door," he ordered Mary.

•

Outside the door, Vargas and Ramos looked at Pone Saiyud, the Thai police officer in charge of the investigating squad that had driven them to the hotel.

"Are you going to break down the door?" Vargas asked.

Saiyud said that presented a problem. The doors of the hotel were made of steel, as part of the fireproofing.

"We'll go in through one of the windows," he said.

Edwards' rooms were on the sixth floor of the seven-story hotel. Two policemen were instructed to go to the roof and lower themselves by rope to the windows.

•

Inside the room, Edwards had put on his shoes. His wife had brought the still sleeping girl from the other room and now, holding Jill in her arms, waited for Edwards to make a decision. They ignored the continuous knocking on the door.

Edwards was indecisive. It was the first time his wife could ever remember seeing him like that. He had always been quick to act before. She attributed it to his being overtired.

Finally he motioned to the two large windows. He told her to look out and see if there was some kind of fire exit. They might be able to sneak out that way.

Mary Edwards took one step toward the windows when there was a crash of breaking glass and a pair of shoes appeared in the broken window. The shoes were immediately followed by legs and the body of a uniformed policeman. A second policeman came in behind him.

Edwards and his wife remained frozen while one of the policemen went to the door and opened it.

Pone Saiyud pointed to Edwards. "Is that your man?"

Vargas and Ramos looked at Edwards, then at each other. "He's our man," they said, almost in unison.

•

There was no need to start extradition proceedings. Edwards was more than willing to go to Venezuela. He correctly thought it would be easier to face a charge of embezzlement in Caracas than to face charges of armed robbery in England.

The next day, Ramos, Vargas, and the Edwards family boarded a plane for Caracas. They arrived in Venezuela on March 12, exactly nineteen days from the day Ramos and Vargas left Caracas to fly to Bogotà. Including the journey back to Venezuela, the police had traveled about twenty-five thousand miles.

Miles Taylor, alias Ralph Edwards, was tried in Caracas and convicted of embezzlement. He was sentenced to prison. His wife was placed on probation so she could take care of their daughter. Police recovered $368,000 of the stolen money.

In December 1974, Taylor was released from prison in Venezuela and extradited to England. He is now serving a ten-year sentence for armed robbery.

Chapter **17**

Narcotics and their abuse are perhaps the largest single source of concern for any country's law-enforcement agencies. Interpol is no exception. It reflects the problems of its member nations. Almost all major cases of drug traffic sooner or later become part of an Interpol investigation. This is because drugs so often cross many borders to reach their point of final sale.

The Interpol department that handles these drug cases is directed by an Englishman with the rank of Detective-Superintendent in Scotland Yard. He has been with Interpol for four years. His department, at present, is the only one to send men into the field. These Interpol men act as advisers to local police. In many instances they have made the difference between solving and not solving a particular case.

A formidable weapon at Interpol's disposal in its battle with drug traffic is the rapid distribution of information concerning known criminals. A good example of this weapon in action netted the police a capture in Greece.

•

On June 15, 1974, a Sunday, the cruise ship *Mimika* docked in the harbor of Rhodes, the largest island of the Dodecanese. Rhodes, which advertises itself as a year-round vacation paradise, was already crowded in June. Hotel accommodations were scarce, the shops were jammed with bargain hunters, and the beaches swarmed with sun-seeking tourists.

The *Mimika* made the run from the mainland three times each week. It stopped at several other islands on its way to Rhodes, picking up passengers and cargo. In a few hours it would leave Rhodes on its return trip to the port of Piraeus.

As usual, it disgorged hordes of people. Most of them came from deck class, where they had spent the eighteen-hour voyage drinking, talking, and playing cards. When they left the ship they were excited, tired, and dirty.

This was not the case with the first-class passengers, who had enjoyed a bed with clean sheets. They came off the ship looking fresh. One of these first-class passengers was a Canadian named Maria Papados. It was her first visit to Greece although both her parents were native Greeks. She had been born and brought up in Toronto, Canada, and had lived there all of her twenty-eight years. Because of her parents, she spoke Greek fluently.

Maria was not planning to stay in the city of Rhodes. Unlike the other visitors, who had come to explore the narrow streets and many shops of the old city, she was anxious to get to Lindos.

Lindos, some thirty-five miles away, is a scenic, undisturbed town with a magnificent beach and an acropolis that overlooks both town and sea.

Maria Papados was not concerned about finding a place to stay in Lindos. She had a friend, Judy Wright, also a Canadian, who had been living in a rented cottage there for over a year, sharing the cottage with her Greek boy friend, Takis Spyrou. Before moving in permanently with Judy, Takis had been an assistant manager of a popular Rhodes discotheque catering to tourists.

Maria hired a taxi to take her to Lindos. She found Judy and Takis eating lunch in front of the cottage. They had been expecting her, and there was a place set at the table for her.

Immediately after greeting them, Maria wanted to know if they had made arrangements to introduce her to the person she had actually come to see. She had important business with that person—narcotics.

The contact was a Greek police sergeant named Alex Kontos. He had been approached and cultivated by Judy and Takis. According to Takis, Kontos needed money and wasn't particular about where it came from. Takis had known him for several years and assured Maria he was reliable.

The next day, Monday, Kontos showed up at the cottage to meet Maria Papados. Maria explained that she and her people needed a transfer point to ship drugs from Lebanon to Canada. Canadian officials were too suspicious of direct shipments. She thought that goods arriving in Canada from Rhodes would pass through Canadian customs more easily.

If it were possible to bring the drugs from Lebanon into Lindos, then take them to the city of Rhodes and ship them out to Canada, she and her friends would be very pleased. It was going to take some help from Kontos, however, to be sure that when the narcotics were put ashore in Lindos nothing would go wrong.

Kontos was not too happy with this. He had been given to understand the narcotics would be sold in Rhodes. He wanted more specific details about why he was so necessary. He pointed out that simply to unload some drugs on the beach at Lindos didn't require his aid.

Maria refused to answer any other questions. She said that someone would be coming in two days who would explain everything in more detail. Her job was to give Kontos a general idea, nothing else. If he wanted to know more, he would have to come back to the cottage on Wednesday afternoon.

Judy and Takis were as much in the dark as Kontos. When he had left to go back to Rhodes, they tried pumping Maria for information, but she told them that they would also have to wait until Wednesday. They, too, had thought the drugs were for distribution in Rhodes.

Wednesday afternoon the group met again. This time there was an additional person, Arthur Regan, a forty-year-old Canadian.

Regan wasted no time on preliminary conversation. He told Kontos that a sailing yacht would pass by Lindos near midnight on June 21. A small boat would be rowed ashore with the drugs—four hundred pounds of heroin. The yacht would dock in the port of Rhodes, just like any other cruising pleasure craft. The drugs would be repackaged in large barrels of cheese. The packing would take place in Lindos, in the cottage. Later, the barrels would be taken to the port of Rhodes and shipped by freighter to Canada.

143

Kontos was to supply another policeman, and together they were to make sure no one disturbed the unloading on the beach at Lindos. Also, Kontos was to purchase four two-hundred-pound barrels of cheese in the city of Rhodes and deliver them to the cottage. For doing these things he would be paid two thousand American dollars.

"What will you pay the man I get to help?" Kontos asked.

Regan told him he would have to pay the other man out of the two thousand. Kontos objected strenuously, and Regan agreed after some argument to give him an extra five hundred. Kontos could pay his helper whatever he chose.

Kontos wanted his money in advance, but Regan was firm on this point. Kontos would be paid, he said, a few days after the shipment left on the freighter, not before. He also told Kontos that there would be several more shipments made in the future.

Kontos agreed to the terms, and the meeting broke up. Kontos was to return sometime the following day with the barrels of cheese. Regan would be leaving Rhodes, and Maria was to be in charge during his absence.

The following morning, Kontos showed up at the cottage with the barrels of cheese. He also brought his promised helper, a policeman named Gus Mathias. Judy, Maria, and Takis began preparing the barrels, and the two policemen went back to Rhodes.

The barrels were made ready for the heroin by emptying half the cheese from each one. This was done so that there was a bottom and top layer of cheese as well as cheese on the sides. To locate the hiding place of the drugs it would be necessary to burrow deep into the cheese. The remaining cheese was buried behind the cottage, as ordered by Maria Papados.

On the night of June 21, Friday, all of them, including the two policemen, went down to the beach to wait for the drugs. Maria had a flashlight with her. The men in the small boat would signal the shore by flashing a light twice, and the shore party would respond the same way if it was safe to come in. If there were any problems, Maria would not respond.

By two in the morning, they decided that for some reason

there wasn't going to be a delivery. Takis wanted to return to the cottage and sleep. Kontos and Mathias wanted to get back to Rhodes. After some discussion Maria prevailed over the group, and it was agreed to remain on the beach all night. When daylight came, they left the beach, angry and tired. But they decided to meet that night and try again. Maria assured them the yacht would certainly show up.

The second night of waiting proved no more successful than the first. No boat was sighted during the long vigil. The grumblings this time were worse than before. Kontos suggested that the yacht had been confiscated for carrying drugs. Takis and Judy were tired of the whole business. They thought Regan might have been arrested. Maria was the only one who still had confidence in the plan. She persuaded Takis and Judy to return for another night's watch, but Kontos and Mathias said they wouldn't come back until they spoke to Regan. If he showed up, then they would believe the drugs were really coming. It was risky for them, they said, to continue taking time from their duties.

Later that afternoon, Maria, Judy, and Takis were sleeping in the cottage when they were awakened by pounding on the door. It was Regan. He was in good spirits and explained the yacht had been delayed in Cyprus, where it had put in for provisions. It would be in Lindos this very night.

"Wasn't that taking a terrible chance, to dock in Cyprus?" Judy asked.

"Not at all," Regan said. It was to make it look as if the yacht was on a normal charter. If anything, it would lend credibility to the reasons for the yacht's appearances in the future.

Takis went to Rhodes to see Kontos. It took him three hours to find the police sergeant, and Kontos said he might have some difficulty getting to Lindos that night. He had drawn all-night duty in police headquarters. It was only after Takis told him Regan had promised them the boat would definitely make an appearance that Kontos said he would try to come.

"You must be there," Takis said.

"I'll try," Kontos replied. "That's all I can say."

Takis returned to Lindos at eight in the evening. He told the others that Kontos might not show up. Regan assured them Kontos would be on hand.

"He'll manage. He needs that money," Regan said.

At eleven, Kontos and Mathias appeared. They were not in a good mood. They were risking disciplinary action and if the drugs didn't arrive that night, it would all be for nothing.

Regan calmed them down, and then they all went to the beach to wait. There were two couples on the beach, and Kontos went to talk to them. In a few minutes they had picked themselves up and left. Kontos was not happy about having to do this. He told Regan that if anything went wrong they would remember him.

"That's what you're being paid for," Regan snapped.

An hour passed, and Kontos nervously pointed out that the yacht hadn't shown up. He told the others that if it didn't come in another hour he was going back to Rhodes. He kept pacing about in small agitated circles.

At ten minutes after twelve, Maria called out. "I think I see it." She pointed out to sea.

The others followed the direction of her outstretched arm with their eyes. There were some lights visible, bobbing up and down in the water. They were moving in the direction of the city of Rhodes on a course parallel to the watchers.

"That's it," Regan announced.

"Maybe it's some other boat," Kontos said. He seemed more nervous than ever.

Regan assured him it was the yacht. He knew the spacing of the lights. It would be too much of a coincidence for it to be another boat the same size at the same time in the same waters. He told them to keep an eye out for the rowboat that would be coming ashore.

In a few minutes Takis called out that he saw something heading for the right side of the beach. The others strained their eyes into the darkness.

Just before the lines of the boat took definite shape, a light flashed toward the beach two times.

Regan returned the signal with Maria's flashlight. Then, leaving Kontos and Mathias on the upper portion of the beach, the rest of the group ran down to meet the boat.

There were three men in the rowboat. As they reached shore, two of them jumped out and beached the boat. With some help from the shore party, four boxes were removed from the boat and placed on the hard sand.

The plan was for the three men to help bring the drugs into the cottage, then to get back in their boat and row to a deserted spot and camp for the night. In midmorning the yacht would return to pick them up.

Three of the boxes were hoisted on the shoulders of the men from the boat. Takis carried the fourth. They began to move in single file up the beach.

Kontos and Mathias came over. Regan told them to go ahead and make sure no one else was around. He was in a hurry to get the drugs into the safety of the cottage.

Ten minutes later the four boxes and the nine people were squeezed into the house. Takis suggested a drink to relax everyone. Regan said no to this. He wanted the boxes emptied and the heroin hidden in the cheese barrels at once. After that, he said, there would be time for drinking.

Suddenly Kontos told everyone to be quiet. He thought he heard something outside the cottage. Almost as he finished speaking, lights flashed against the curtained windows.

"What the hell is that?" Regan yelled.

Kontos told him to be quiet. He and Mathias would go outside and investigate. It might be some kids fooling around. He would get rid of them in a hurry.

Regan wanted to hide the boxes. They began to move them under a bed. Kontos told them to stop. They were making too much noise, he explained. It was better to let him and Mathias go outside. Had they forgotten that he and Mathias were policemen?

"Whatever it is, I can take care of it," Kontos said.

He opened the door and stepped outside.

Chapter 18

In February 1974, the National Central Bureau of Egypt was informed by Interpol that large-scale drug traffic was taking place between Lebanon and Syria and that the persons responsible for this were from Cairo. An informer had supplied the names of two men, Salah Ali and Mahmoud Ahmed.

The Egyptian antinarcotic service made an immediate investigation and found out that heroin was being smuggled into Egypt and stored in Ahmed's tourist shop. The shop was a place frequented by many Europeans and Americans. Along with souvenir items, Ahmed sold various types of sweets from all over the Middle East.

The police raided the store on March 10 and discovered more than 150 pounds of heroin concealed in wooden boxes. The boxes contained sweets, but their sides had been cleverly altered to provide space for the heroin. Ahmed and Ali were promptly arrested and the shop closed.

When the National Central Bureau of Lebanon was told of the arrests in Cairo, they conducted an investigation in Beirut that led to the arrest of five persons. Among those arrested were the makers of the wooden boxes.

These men explained that the procedure was to hide the heroin in the boxes along with vegetables. The vegetables would then be shipped to Damascus, Syria, where they would be replaced by sweets, Next, the boxes would be loaded onto a cargo ship and sent to Cairo via Alexandria. These elaborate precautions were taken to get past suspicious customs officers.

The police wanted to know the original source of the heroin. None of the arrested people could or would say. The only information they gave the police was that a Canadian named Jack Ross was the contact for the drugs when they first came to Lebanon.

The National Central Bureau of Canada tried to find out something about a Jack Ross. It quickly became obvious that the name was an alias. Canada had no record of a passport issued in that name, nor was there any information on the name in their police files. They did what they could. Using the physical description of Ross supplied by the men arrested in the Middle East, they began a quiet search among known and suspected narcotics dealers to see if any of them matched the description. They also kept Interpol Headquarters in St. Cloud informed of their progress.

•

During the time the Canadians were investigating, police in Athens made an arrest involving ten persons aboard a charter yacht, registered in Turkey. The boat was impounded in the Greek port of Piraeus and the persons aboard charged with attempting to smuggle heroin into Greece. The amount was two hundred pounds.

In the susequent investigation it was learned that the contact man for the drugs was named Jack Ross, a Canadian, according to the men from the boat. They believed he was not just a contact man but also a key figure behind the operation. They described him to the Greek authorities, who forwarded the description to Canada. This description was the same as the Canadians had received earlier.

The General Secretariat was furnished the information and asked to aid in whatever way possible in finding Ross. Interpol had nothing under that name in its files. However, Interpol has a special file designed to help identify persons by the type of crime and methods employed in committing that crime. This file revealed that a man named Arthur Regan had twice been arrested in drug cases and both times had used boats passed off as charter boats to transport drugs. He had spent two years in prison the first time and three years the second. He had been released from a Mexican prison the last time in September 1972. They suggested that the Canadian Police find Regan and question him. Regan seemed to fit the physical description of Jack Ross.

Canada-Interpol replied to the General Secretariat in a few days. Regan was not in the country. They believed he was in Damascus or Beirut. Copies of his photograph were sent to Greece and to Lebanon, where it was established that Ross was an alias being used by Regan.

A red notice was issued on June 5 for the arrest of Regan. On June 6, however, an informer in Toronto told police that a Maria Papados was involved in a large drug deal and she would be contacting Regan somewhere in the Middle East.

A police check discovered that Maria Papados had tickets for a round-trip flight to Athens. It was decided not to arrest Regan but to let him continue with whatever plans he had made. The police now hoped that Regan would not be picked up until the information about Maria Papados had reached all the National Central Bureaus that were looking for him.

Regan was found in Beirut, but fortunately the police had the second message. He was kept under surveillance there while Maria Papados was being watched in Toronto.

She had an arrest record—three charges of narcotic violations. She had never been convicted—yet. Her photograph and fingerprints were sent to the General Secretariat and in turn distributed to the National Central Bureaus. When she arrived in Athens the police picked up her trail and wired Rhodes as soon as she boarded the *Mimika* on June 14.

•

In Rhodes, Police Sergeant Alex Kontos had discussed with his colonel the fact that Takis Spyrou had approached him with an offer to make some easy money. Along with Spyrou, there had been a Canadian girl, Judy Wright. They had not told him exactly what they had in mind, but he strongly suspected it might have to do with drugs. He had known Takis when Takis had worked in a Rhodes night club and been friendly with him because he suspected Takis was selling drugs to tourists. He had never been able to prove anything, but he had stayed on good terms with Takis over the years, waiting for some evidence to confirm his suspicions.

Since he had been told by Takis and the girl that he would be meeting someone in mid-June to discuss the project, his colonel had told him to play along. Now, with the information that Maria Papados was coming to Rhodes, they decided that probably this was the person Kontos was to meet. He was instructed to agree to whatever was suggested and appear a willing partner.

That same Saturday that Maria Papados got on the *Mimika*, Takis informed Kontos that he should come to Lindos, to the cottage, to meet and talk over the proposition. He was to come on Monday.

After the meeting that included Maria, Kontos returned to Rhodes to inform his superiors of the drug-shipment plan. The police were very interested to learn that another person was expected. They were sure it would turn out to be Arthur Regan.

Lebanon reported that Regan was on his way to Athens, with a connecting flight to Rhodes. The police were ordered not to interfere with Regan but to let him go where he wanted. He would, of course, be kept under constant surveillance.

After the Wednesday-afternoon meeting at which Kontos met and recognized Regan, a problem arose. Regan had said he was leaving Rhodes. The police had to decide if they should arrest him before he left. They would be able to intercept the drug shipment in Lindos. It wasn't necessary to let Regan roam around anymore.

They finally decided to let Regan go. He could be picked up at any time, they thought. And wherever he went, the police would know his exact movements.

Kontos went ahead and, with Gus Mathias, purchased the cheese Regan had ordered and took it to Lindos the next day. As far as the two policemen could tell, they were completely trusted, which, in fact, they were.

The police went on with their plans. While Kontos and

Mathias were on the beach waiting for the narcotics, a squad of armed policemen would be waiting on the outskirts of Lindos. They would move in only after the group with the heroin was inside the cottage.

So it happened that on that first night when the fruitless vigil was kept, unknown to all but Kontos and Mathias, ten policemen were also keeping watch. They were just as disappointed as the group on the beach.

When the second night came to an end without any boat arriving, the police regretted not having made an arrest of Regan and all his crowd on charges of conspiring to smuggle narcotics into Greece. However, later that day they got word that Regan was on his way back.

When Takis came into town to tell Kontos that Regan was back and the drugs really on their way, Kontos was well aware of it.

The reason he and Mathias didn't arrive in Lindos until eleven that night was that they were taking part in a long conference about what to do if the boat failed to show again. The decision was made to arrest the group anyway.

Once more, while Kontos and Mathias were on the beach waiting, ten policemen kept watch with them. They saw the signal from the rowboat and at once began to make their way toward the cottage.

When the rowboat came in and the drugs were brought ashore, Kontos and his partner stayed on the upper part of the beach as ordered by Regan. Unwittingly he had given them a little time to discuss the situation. Although they were certain the other police had seen the signal and were getting into position near the cottage, they were somewhat anxious. Mathias pointed out that, since they were unarmed, if a problem arose before help reached them there wasn't much they could do. He thought he might be able to contact the police now and return before he was missed. Kontos was against this. They would have to believe the waiting police had seen the signal. They moved down the beach toward the group that was in the process of bringing the boxes to the cottage.

At the moment when the lights began to shine into the cottage and Kontos moved to open the door and step outside, Regan, with an instinct that something was about to happen that he wouldn't like, had moved next to a window.

Almost at the instant that Kontos disappeared into the night, police burst into the cottage with guns in their hands. Regan, at the same time, dove through the window, scrambled to his feet, and raced for the beach.

A few shots were fired after him, and two officers set out in pursuit. Inside the cottage, everyone was quickly handcuffed and, along with the drugs, made ready to be taken to Rhodes by police van. The van was brought up to the cottage, but the police decided to wait for Regan to be brought back before starting the trip.

Regan was not to take that ride that night. He had shown more speed of foot than the police thought possible. The men pursuing him got to the water's edge in time to see him rowing energetically away, already some twenty-five yards from shore. They fired at the boat, but it made a poor target in the water. They rejoined the others, and the news of Regan's escape was radioed to Rhodes.

There wasn't much Regan could do with a rowboat. The police thought he would probably beach it somewhere nearby and try to make his way unobserved to Rhodes, where he would attempt to charter a small boat to take him to Turkey. Or, they reasoned, he might try to hide out near some small village and see if he could make a deal with a local fisherman. A search party was organized under the supervision of Kontos, and they set off at once along the shoreline in the direction Regan had begun to row. If they hurried, they thought, they had a chance to get him when he tried to come to shore. They were certain they could travel faster on land than Regan could by rowboat. They were wrong.

While the pursuers hurried along the shoreline, the police van containing Takis Spyrou, Maria Papados, Judy Wright, and the three men who'd landed in the rowboat, started for Rhodes. Four policemen went with them. The rest had joined in the hunt for Regan.

Kontos and his party spotted the empty rowboat floating in the water near Pefki, a tiny village on the other side of a point of land separating Lindos from Pefki. If they hadn't followed the shoreline the distance would have been about two and a half miles. It was closer to five beside the water, but they had wanted to stay in sight of the sea in case Regan doubled back.

There was a small road leading from Pefki to the main highway to Rhodes. It was a little more than two miles to the highway and the police split into two groups. One would follow the road toward the highway,the other would search in the general area of Pefki and gradually extend its search in a direction away from Rhodes.

By daylight, Regan had not been found. By this time additional police had come from Rhodes for a full-scale manhunt.

The airport and the harbor in Rhodes had been alerted during the night. Police were posted everywhere by morning. There was not a place on the island that Regan could show himself to get transportation out of Rhodes.

For two days the search continued. There was still no trace of Regan. Because of the large crowd of tourists in Rhodes, it was necessary for some of the police to stop looking and come back to the city. It was decided to leave certain places, such as roads leading to inhabited areas, under constant watch. The airport and harbors were also watched. There was confidence that when Regan surfaced he would be caught quickly.

Through the Interpol network, all National Central Bureaus were alerted just in case Regan should somehow get away from Rhodes. He would find no place safe for him. His photograph and fingerprints were in the offices of 120 National Central Bureaus.

Friday, June 28, at ten in the morning, a complaint was phoned in to police headquarters in the city of Rhodes. A shopkeeper stated that a man had just eaten a large meal in his restaurant and left without paying the bill. His description of the man fitted Regan. The police could scarcely believe it. They hadn't thought it possible for Regan to get into the city without being caught.

The restaurant was in the old city, behind walls. Police were posted at all exits, and another four police groups were sent into the old city to hunt Regan, if it was Regan indeed who had caused the phone call.

Two hours later, an officer posted at one of the exits was giving directions to some tourists when he observed a man moving toward the arched exit.

The man had caught the officer's eye because of his torn and dirty clothing. The policeman, Petros Fontinis, called to the man in Greek, ordering him to stop. When his call was ignored he repeated it in English. The man broke into a run.

Fontinis ran after him. The man ran slowly, and Fontinis, a young athletic type, overtook him easily. He put a hand on the man's shoulder, stopping him, then spun him around. One look at the man's face was all Fontinis needed. He knew he was holding Arthur Regan.

•

With the arrest of Regan, a carefully laid supply line of illegal drugs, stretching from Burma to Canada, was snapped. Using information obtained from Regan, a total of twenty-four arrests were made in Asia, Europe, the Middle East, and North America.

Arthur Regan, Maria Papados, Takis Spyrou, Judy Wright, and the three men from the rowboat were tried and convicted of smuggling narcotics into Greece. They are now serving prison sentences in that country.

The crew of the yacht was also arrested and sentenced to prison terms. The yacht was impounded by the Greek government.

Because Interpol was able to identify Regan from one of its special files, police were able to destroy a drug ring even before it was fully in operation.

Chapter 19

It is a fairly well known fact that the police rely on informers for a great deal of their information about criminal activity. Informers are made, rarely found. The police recruit them when they are particularly susceptible. Simply stated, when the police have enough hard facts to jail a criminal, they may offer him a deal. If he accepts and acts in the role of informer, he stays out of prison. If he refuses, he goes behind bars.

The police-informer relationship is a precarious one for the criminal. He is between the ax the police hold figuratively over his head and the more literal ax his friends may use on his head if they find out about his police contacts.

The authorities defend this system by pointing to statistics. Crime is rising at an alarming rate. In their war against crime, the police are losing ground. They need all the help they can get.

Not quite all their informers are recruited. Every so often one turns up on his own, hoping to trade information for protection or some other favor. In such cases, a gold mine of information may be unearthed. This was the case when the police in Savannah, Georgia, made what appeared to be a routine narcotics arrest. However, the story does not begin in Savannah. It begins in France.

·

Bertrand Lefebvre had been fascinated by airplanes and aviation ever since he was a child. His continuing dream, while he grew up in the Paris suburb of Suresnes, was to become an airline pilot. He never quite made it, but he did get as close to his dream as his skills allowed. He ended up with a job as a *commissaire de bord*, or purser, for the international flights of Air France.

By anyone's estimate except his own, he had a well-paid and interesting job. His regular run was from Paris to Buenos Aires. He saved himself from the boredom he felt by performing a service that was not part of his job. He transported drugs—heroin, to be exact—each time he made the flight. He carried the drugs in a false bottom of his suitcase.

After two years, Lefebvre had begun to consider himself indispensable to the drug ring. He could not have been more wrong. He was actually regarded as a small cog in the overall operation, and if he'd known how expendable he was, he would not have been nearly so tranquil when he arrived for a certain evening's flight.

Before checking in, he had to meet a man named José Lapora. The place selected for the meeting was near one of the elevators of the underground parking lot. Lapora was the man who had recruited him to transport the narcotics two years earlier. Since that time, Lefebvre had seen Lapora just twice, so he knew this meeting must mean something important had come up.

He had time to smoke one cigarette before he saw Lapora approaching the elevator. Lapora was a tall man with gray hair and a commanding presence. He was, on this night as usual, immaculately dressed in an expensive business suit. He had just a few words to say to Lefebvre.

"This is the last trip we need you to make for us. We'll be using another method from now on. Don't try to contact us again."

Lefebvre was stunned. He tried to ask for an explanation but Lapora told him that no explanation was needed. The only other thing he did say was that Lefebvre was to forget he had ever done business for him. Then he turned abruptly away and left a puzzled and unhappy Lefebvre behind.

Lefebvre didn't know it but he was not the only person to hear that piece of news. Three other pursers who had been doing the same thing had been dismissed as well. Lefebvre hadn't known that anyone else was transporting drugs but himself. The thing he did know was that his income was due to take a hefty slide.

He had no time to run after Lapora. He had to get ready for his flight. However, he made up his mind to ignore what he'd been told and to contact Lapora when he returned from Argentina. He wasn't about to let go of his opportunity to make the extra money without a struggle.

·

The organization José Lapora worked for and, in fact, ran was a large one. It involved a chain of contacts that reached to the "Golden Triangle," that part of the world comprising Burma, Laos, and Thailand, where the bulk of the raw opium originated. One of Lapora's lieutenants was stationed in Marseilles, where the opium was processed before being sent up to Paris for distribution. In Buenos Aires, a group which was also under the supervision of one of Lapora's aides distributed the drugs throughout South America.

Because Lapora had a real genius for organization, none of the people working for him had even come close to being caught during the two-year period of operation. In fact, the control was so good that although Lefebvre and the other three pursers knew each other well, none of them knew that the others were employed by Lapora. Each one thought he was the only courier.

Although the business was very profitable, Lapora was not the type of man to stick with one method if an even better and cheaper one could be found to move his merchandise. He had been working with some fresh ideas for a few months and finally had come across the needed contacts to ensure the success of his new plan.

Since he was very thorough, he first had to turn his attention to phasing out his old method before starting with the new one. The couriers had become expensive, and as part of the original group they knew too much. The easiest way to dismiss them was to have them killed. At the time Lapora spoke to Lefebvre in the underground parking lot, orders had already gone out to dispose of the other couriers. For Lefebvre, a mishap was to occur in Buenos Aires.

The new method for shipping the drugs was a simple one. Lapora had recruited one of the mechanics who worked on the big jets. This mechanic would remove a plate from the fuselage of the aircraft and conceal the narcotics behind it. On the plane's arrival in Buenos Aires, another mechanic would again remove the plate and take the shipment. To bring the drugs into the airport and then to take them away at the other end, he had recruited men working for the food concessionaires who serviced the airlines.

What especially pleased Lapora was that the cost of this system came to exactly half of the cost of the couriers, while at the same time the quantity of drugs shipped came to double the old amount.

•

Air France Flight 095 took off on schedule at 6:55 P.M. It would stop in both Nice and Dakar before winging over the Atlantic toward Argentina. It was due to land at Ezeiza International Airport, outside of Buenos Aires, at 8 A.M. the next morning.

It was a good flight, without turbulence, and enjoyable for everyone aboard except Bertrand Lefebvre. He was far from stupid and had begun to think about what Lapora had said. It occurred to him that it might not be safe for him in France. He was aware of the ruthless planning Lapora was capable of. There was the case of one man found shot through the head who Lefebvre was certain had worked for Lapora. The case had never been solved.

By the time the flight was nearly over, Lefebvre had made up his mind that he would have to leave France and find another place to live. It would be too easy for Lapora to have him killed, especially if he was no longer going to be part of the operation.

At the airport, after checking through the Air France operations section, Lefebvre was met by his Argentine contact, Ramon Estes.

Since it was about a twenty-five-mile drive into Buenos Aires, Estes customarily met the couriers. Lefebvre and Estes had become friends during the time that Lefebvre had been transporting the drugs. Often, during the layover, the two of them went out together.

When he got into Estes' car this time, Lefebvre was greeted warmly. Estes evidently didn't know that he was making his last delivery. At least that's what Lefebvre thought. If he had had the slightest idea that the man next to him who was smiling so amiably had been designated as his executioner, Lefebvre would have been much more nervous than he already was.

As Estes' car joined the traffic heading for the city, Estes told Lefebvre that he was going to introduce him to some good friends. Those friends, meanwhile, were making plans for where to dispose of Lefebvre's body. Estes' instructions had been to take Lefebvre to an apartment where two members of Lapora's local organization who acted as enforcers would shoot him.

They never reached the apartment. Ten minutes after they left the airport, the right front tire of Estes' car blew out. Estes lost control of the vehicle. It spun off the highway, flipped over, and came to rest upside down.

Lefebvre was unhurt, but Ramon Estes had been flung out of the car. Even while other cars were stopping and people rushed toward them, Lefebvre got to Estes' side. Estes was dead. His head split open by a rock, he lay in a grotesque position, his unseeing eyes staring up into the sun.

Soon the police and an ambulance joined the crowd of onlookers. Estes' body was taken into the ambulance, and Lefebvre, along with his valuable suitcase, was driven into the city to a hotel.

Lefebvre didn't have any place to deliver the drugs. He had no other contact in Buenos Aires. While sitting in his hotel room he decided to put the suitcase with the drugs in storage. He would return to Paris, take his money from his bank, get a month's leave from the airline, and use the time to find himself a new identity and a new country. Later, he would be able to return to Buenos Aires and pick up the suitcase. The one thing he knew he would not do was to contact Lapora or anyone else connected with the organization.

•

In Paris, José Lapora learned of Estes' death three days after Lefebvre returned to France. At the same time, he learned that Lefebvre was still alive. This bothered him. His new operation had just made its first run, and it proved to be exactly what he had hoped for. It was all the more reason for Lefebvre to be found and done in. He said so to his chief lieutenant, Antonio Gaspera. An immediate search was begun for Lefebvre, and the organization posted a reward of ten thousand American dollars payable to the man who killed their quarry. Lapora settled down to wait. He was sure the matter would be settled within a few days.

•

Even if Lefebvre had known any of this, it probably would not have changed his plans. After his return, he had taken his money, arranged his time off from the airline, and gone to Amsterdam. There he made arrangements to get a false passport and identity card. While he waited, he holed up in an inexpensive hotel room.

During the two weeks before he got his new papers, he had time to formulate a concrete scheme. First he would go to Argentina and get his narcotics. He would sell them there. He was certain he could find a buyer. After that he would have enough money to go to New York and get involved in the drug business there. He spoke enough English, he felt, to get by. Also, since New York was such a big city it seemed like an excellent place to drop out of sight. He was still fearful of Lapora, but he thought that Lapora had no business in the United States and so he would be safe there. Lefebvre was later to admit that at this time he was so confused that he never asked himself if it would be an easy thing to break into the rackets in a strange country.

His worst moments came when he arrived in Buenos Aires. He was afraid someone would recognize him at the airport. He even thought that perhaps some of Lapora's men would be looking for him because of the drugs he had not returned.

He was lucky, however, and had no problems. He got his

suitcase out of storage and within the week had made a contact and sold the heroin.

Using his new passport, he had no difficulty when he arrived in the United States. Although he was to say that he felt everyone was looking for him, at that time, of course, no one except Lapora's men was looking. Lefebvre was not on any police wanted list.

Shortly after coming to New York, he made the acquaintance of a small-time drug dealer named Eric Rouse. He and Rouse decided to throw in together. Rouse claimed to have many good contacts, and Lefebvre told Rouse he could raise some capital if he needed it. He might not have been so taken with Rouse if he had known that Rouse was under almost constant surveillance by the New York City Police.

•

Meanwhile, Lapora was raking in the money. His organization had expanded dramatically. He could count forty-five people directly on his payroll. In one month he had moved eight hundred pounds of heroin by air freight, his style, and had made plans to increase his shipments.

He began to think seriously about widening his markets. The obvious place to look was the United States. He thought enough of the idea to take a trip to New York, accompanied by Gaspera.

In New York he contacted three well-established dealers. They told him they would be happy to handle anything he could send in. They wanted him to begin shipments at once. This Lapora would not do. He wanted the same kind of operation in the States that he had in Paris and Buenos Aires. He returned to France but left Gaspera behind to try to find an airport contact either in New York or Miami.

Back in Paris, Lapora raised the price on Lefebvre's head to twenty thousand dollars. It was just good business practice, he felt. He couldn't afford a link that was out of place and might cause him trouble later on.

•

Just about the time Lapora had flown back to France, Rouse informed Lefebvre that he had been given some

162

interesting information about a shipment of raw opium coming into Tampa. What did Lefebvre think about going down to Florida and checking it out?

Lefebvre thought it sounded good. He and Rouse made arrangements to be in Tampa two days before the freighter that carried the opium was due to dock.

They made one mistake. They had their final discussion about their Florida trip in a crowded bar. Some people overheard them. Among these people was a police informer. He didn't know how good the information was, but he did have the name of the ship. He gave it to the police along with the rest of what he had heard. As he knew neither Rouse nor Lefebvre, he was not able to give the police any names.

Rouse and Lefebvre left on schedule and, as luck would have it, Rouse was not being watched that day. If the police had known he was flying to Florida he would have been met at the Tampa airport, and what followed probably would not have happened. As it was, the two arrived in Tampa, quickly found their contact, a Chinese seaman, and were able to begin negotiating for the opium.

Chapter 20

The police in Tampa had received a warning call from the New York City Police to be on the lookout for a freighter called the *Markus*, under Liberian registration. They could expect it to be carrying illicit drugs. The New York Police suggested the drugs were opium. They couldn't vouch for the validity of their information. It had been supplied by a not-too-reliable informer.

The Tampa Police decided to act on the information. They made the necessary arrangements to keep the ship and its crew under watch when the ship came into port. At the same time, two government narcotics agents made preparations to try to negotiate for the drugs.

The two agents, posing as interested buyers, began to speak to the crew of the ship and let it be known they knew opium was on board and were interested in making a purchase. The crew, which was mostly Chinese, treated this approach with caution. However, three of the Chinese seamen admitted they could get their hands on thirty pounds of raw opium if they were offered a good price.

The agents, trying to impress upon the seamen that they were serious prospects for the narcotics, drove such a hard bargain that the ship sailed for its next port of call, Savannah, before anything was settled.

Although Tampa Police were aware of the ship's sailing date, they had no specialist available to conduct a search of the freighter. They were afraid that if they tried to look themselves, the narcotics would be too well hidden or else dumped over the side before they got their hands on them. It seemed a better move to inform the Savannah Police and let them prepare to make the seizure.

One reason the agents had such a hard time trying to buy the opium was because of Rouse and Lefebvre. Those two had been told by their contact in Tampa that others were also making negotiations. Rouse, who had a naturally suspicious nature, suggested that their competitors might be agents. This idea was passed on to the crew and helped to make them very hard to deal with.

Rouse and Lefebvre were told to go to Savannah and arrange to buy the opium there. They were given the name of another contact, also Chinese, and told that he would meet them when they got there.

When the freighter docked in Savannah, the police were ready for it. They had the dock under watch before the ship's arrival at 4 A.M. At ten that morning a taxi pulled up on the dock and a Chinese man got out and boarded the freighter. He left about an hour later with one of the seamen. They took a taxi to a hotel in the city, and the police followed them, leaving a man to keep watch on them.

About four hours later, police watching the ship saw five crewmen, all Chinese, disembark. A taxi took them to the same hotel the other two men had gone to. The police called for reinforcements, and when they had arrived, they raided the hotel room.

Fifty-two bags of raw opium were seized. The seven Chinese were arrested, and along with the Chinese the police also arrested Rouse and Lefebvre. Those two had sixteen thousand dollars with them to buy the narcotics.

Taken to the police station, all were questioned by the local police and also by government agents. The Chinese refused to say anything. They were willing to sit silently and let the police prove whatever they could. That was not the case, however, with either Rouse or Lefebvre.

Rouse, of course, couldn't tell the police very much for the simple reason that he didn't know much. He was only trying to show that he was cooperative, since he had so many prior convictions he didn't want to appear in front of a judge without a good word from the police.

Lefebvre, on the other hand, began by explaining that the name he had been using in the United States, Jean Lajoie, was not his own. He went on to talk about his involvement with Rouse. The police didn't get very interested until he began to explain about his job in France on the airplanes. He was careful not to give too many details until he had really whetted their interest. Then he offered to tell all he knew if they would let him off the hook. He pointed out that as the police had caught him before he had actually exchanged money for opium, they might have a tough time proving much in court. True, he admitted, they might get him on a conspiracy charge and also for illegal entry because of his false identification, but, all things considered, he was in a position to give them a lot of valuable information in exchange for his freedom.

The Savannah Police turned him over to the federal agents. They had only local authority and felt the government men could make better use of Lefebvre. The agents made a quick call to the Treasury Department, specifically to Interpol-U.S.A. Before making any definite decisions they wanted Lefebvre thoroughly checked out to see if he was telling them the truth about himself.

Interpol-U.S.A. contacted Interpol-France and requested all available facts on Lefebvre. They received an answer in two days, while Lefebvre was taken to Washington in federal custody. As soon as the agents were sure that Lefebvre was indeed in a position to give them some important information, they exchanged ideas with Interpol-France to decide the best way to use what they had.

By the end of the week they were ready to offer Lefebvre a deal. It was nothing close to what he had expected. What they wanted him to do was to contact the leaders of the organization in France and set a police trap for them. If he did this, the United States was willing to drop charges against him. The French took the position that they would decide what to do after they broke up the drug ring. They were promising Lefebvre nothing in advance. The only definite promise they made was that, if he wouldn't cooperate, after he finished his time in an American prison they would bring him back to France and put him in prison there.

Lefebvre was frightened. He explained that he had only one contact. It was a number he had been instructed to call in Paris if he had any problems. In Argentina, he explained, his one contact, Roman Estes, was dead. He wanted to know if the police understood that the organization knew he had kept the drugs he was supposed to deliver. Did the police have any idea what they would do to him for that?

Yes, the police understood everything. In fact, the French Police didn't mind informing him that the bodies of three pursers had been found. If what he had said about transporting drugs was true, they had probably been fired the same way he had been. He was lucky to be alive. However, they were not interested in all that. All they wanted to know was whether or not he was going to work for them.

Lefebvre agreed. He was at once whisked to France and introduced to the man who would be his police contact. The officer was inspector Raoul Beauchamp, a member of a flying squad whose duties were to investigate important narcotics crimes.

Beauchamp explained to Lefebvre that he would give Lefebvre as much protection as possible. The first thing he wanted him to do was to set up a meeting with the people who had the phone number that Lefebvre was supposed to use in an emergency. The police had checked out the number and found it was listed to a young woman, an Argentinian national named Maria Sanchez. Beauchamp was certain she could get in touch with someone in the gang if there was a good reason. As he saw it, the appearance of Lefebvre would prove good enough.

Interpol-Argentina was contacted and given the name of Maria Sanchez to work on. They were also brought up to date about Lefebvre, of course, and his relationship with Ramon Estes. The police of both Argentina and France were now concentrating on the case.

Lefebvre called the phone number while the police monitored the call. He gave a code word to identify himself when Maria Sanchez answered. She told him to call back in three hours. When he did, with the police again listening, he was told to come to her apartment the following afternoon at two o'clock.

Lefebvre had reservations about going. He was sure he would be killed. "They're only setting me up. That's why they made the appointment," he told Beauchamp.

Beauchamp told him not to worry. The police were not going to take any chances on losing him. They would start an immediate stakeout of the apartment. It would remain in effect through the time of the meeting the next day. If any rough characters showed up they would be stopped. Also, there would be two policemen on guard on the same floor as the apartment. They would be able to come to Lefebvre's help if anything went wrong inside.

When Lefebvre showed up and was let into the apartment, he found himself alone with Maria Sanchez. She told him at once that the people she represented wanted the heroin back, if he still had it, or the money if he didn't.

Lefebvre had been prepared for this by Beauchamp. He explained to the girl that he still had the drugs and wanted nothing better than to return them if they would guarantee nothing would happen to him.

Maria Sanchez said she would contact her people and he could call back later in the day to receive instructions. Now, Lefebvre, continuing to obey orders, asked if she could arrange a meeting between him and Lapora. She said she didn't know anyone by that name. He said he would call later for the promised instructions, and left the apartment.

Beauchamp told him that while he'd been inside the police had spotted two men who were evidently supposed to keep him in sight. They had followed Lefebvre but had been intercepted by the police and questioned. The police had deliberately questioned them about something they had no connection with, then let them go. It had delayed them long enough so that they lost track of Lefebvre.

Lefebvre made the next call to Maria Sanchez and was told to place the drugs in a suitcase, then put it in a locker located in the Gare du Nord. The key to the locker was to be given to a man who would contact him in the station as soon as he walked away from the locker. The man would ask him where to find the train to Lille. To be sure the timing was correct, Lefebvre was to enter the Gare du Nord at exactly 8 P.M., by the station clock.

"And am I guaranteed safety?" Lefebvre asked.

He was told if he followed instructions he would have nothing further to worry about. All they wanted was to get back what was theirs.

A suitcase was procured for Lefebvre, and once more men were posted by the police. They planned to follow the man who took the key from Lefebvre. It looked as if they would begin to get some results.

At eight that evening, Lefebvre walked into the railroad station to the lockers situated in the central entrance. He found an empty one, placed the suitcase inside, and walked slowly away toward the exit. A short man wearing a stocking cap came up to him and asked him in a low voice where he could find the train to Lille. Lefebvre held out the key and the man took it, spun on his heel, and walked out into the street. Lefebvre, doing what he had been told by Beauchamp, went to the stairway leading to the Métro and went down toward the underground trains.

The police following the man in the stocking cap watched him board a number 49 bus. One of the officers got on as well and followed him when he got off at the Gare St. Lazare.

From that station the man took a local train and exited at La Défense, the police officer still behind him. The man now went on foot toward one of the new high-rise apartment houses and dropped the key into a mail slot. The officer was unable to see which one since it would have meant getting too close.

The officer did the next best thing. He stopped the man on his way out of the apartment house lobby and placed him under arrest.

Under questioning, the man in the stocking cap gave one name to Inspector Beauchamp. It was an important name, the name of the man to whom he had delivered the key. It was Antonio Gaspera.

The police ran a quick check on Gaspera but found nothing on him in their files in Paris. They could only come up with the fact that he was an Argentinian with permission to stay in France for one year. He had a visitor's card issued by the Préfecture de Nanterre. His occupation was listed as business consultant. Interpol-France at once sent a high-priority message to Buenos Aires to request information on Gaspera.

Things were getting tight for Beauchamp. He was sure that within the next twenty-four hours someone would come into the Gare du Nord to pick up the suitcase. They would find it empty and know at once that the police were after them. Beauchamp decided to pick up the man who came for the suitcase. At least, if nothing else, the organization might be led to believe that their man had taken off with the drugs. It would buy the police some time while they continued investigating.

At eleven in the morning of the next day, two things occurred almost at the same time. The man who came for the suitcase was taken into custody, and Interpol-Argentina replied to Interpol-France, informing them that Antonio Gaspera was well known to the police, with many arrests for drug violations. He had been out of Argentina for three years and was wanted for questioning by the Buenos Aires Police concerning an unsolved murder. He was not the suspect but a highly regarded material witness.

The police in Buenos Aires had some other news. They had taken an airplane mechanic into custody, and this man had told them that he regularly took packages of heroin from a hiding place in the fuselage of large jet aircraft. He did not know who was sending the stuff. His job was to get it and pass it on. The man he passed it to had also been arrested. This second man worked for a food-service company that did business with the airlines. Since the planes carrying the heroin came from France, the French police were asked to investigate at their end. Lapora's business was beginning to crumble at its foundations.

Gaspera was arrested within the hour at his apartment and confronted by Lefebvre. He was not known by name to Lefebvre, but Lefebvre knew him by sight. He had seen him on three occasions. On one of them, Gaspera had delivered the drugs to Lefebvre.

Gaspera did not prove cooperative. He refused to say anything to either confirm or deny Lefebvre's story. He was held in custody pending further investigation.

Even as Gaspera was taken by the police, other officers acting on the information supplied by Interpol-Argentina were making arrests of three persons. Two were men who worked for a food concessionaire. They were caught in the act of bringing packages of heroin into the airport for delivery to a mechanic, François Durant, whose job it was to place the drugs on the planes going to Buenos Aires.

Durant was brought in to see Beauchamp and revealed the fact that he had a meeting scheduled with a high-ranking member of the drug ring that same evening. He didn't know the man's name but when he described him, Lefebvre was able to state that he thought it was José Lapora.

The police decided that Lapora wanted to see Durant because he must have heard about what had happened in Argentina. He might want to change his method of operation or even stop it for some time, and he probably wanted to inform Durant about this.

The police decided to let Durant keep the meeting. They, along with Lefebvre, who would be there to make a positive identification, would go along. The meeting was to be at nine in the evening in the underground parking lot of Orly Airport, near the bottom-floor elevators.

At the appointed time, the police were ready. Durant stood, his back to the elevator doors, and waited. At five minutes after nine, Lefebvre, crouched behind a car, told Beauchamp that the man walking toward Durant was Lapora.

Beauchamp gave the prearranged signal and the police

converged on Lapora. At first he tried to bluff his way out of the situation by claiming he was a businessman on the way to catch a plane. The police were making a grave error, he said. He stopped trying to talk his way out when he saw Lefebvre.

Lapora refused to say anything until he was confronted with Antonio Gaspera. By this time Gaspera had decided to cooperate with the police. They induced this change of mind in Gaspera by telling him he was going to face a charge of murder. The police were referring to the murdered pursers. Gaspera said he had had nothing to do with arranging that, but he knew who was responsible and would be glad to tell them about it.

Now, facing his employer, he told the police that it was Lapora who had ordered the murders. Lapora denied the accusation, turning it on Gaspera. Before things got out of hand, the two men were taken to separate cells and locked up. As far as the police were concerned, they had all the time they would need to finish their investigation of the case.

When the final tally was in, it was impressive. In Argentina, police arrested six persons in connection with the case. All six were convicted of illicit traffic in drugs and sentenced to prison.

In Marseilles, four persons were arrested and eventually sentenced to prison, also in connection with the case. It was in Marseilles that the opium was processed, and the laboratory was discovered and closed down. Three hundred pounds of opium were seized there by the investigating police.

Eleven other persons were arrested in Burma, Laos, and Thailand. These people were found on the strength of information given to the police through the Interpol network. They also were sentenced to prison for their part in the affair.

In the Paris area, seven persons, whose names were given to the police by Gaspera and Lapora, were arrested and convicted of illicit drug trafficking. They were also imprisoned.

José Lapora, Antonio Gaspera, and a third person, Francisco Provato, were charged with murder. The prosecution failed to get a guilty verdict in the murder case due to lack of evidence. The three men were then tried on charges of illicit traffic in narcotics and sentenced to lengthy prison terms.

Maria Sanchez was extradited to Argentina, where she was convicted on a prior narcotics charge and imprisoned.

François Durant and the two men who brought him the drugs were all sentenced to prison terms for illicit traffic in narcotics.

Bertrand Lefebvre was sentenced to six months in prison for his part in the affair and on his release was placed on five years' probation. The lightness of his sentence was due to his cooperation with the authorities.

In all, thirty-six persons were arrested, tried, and convicted. More importantly, drug traffic that had reached a figure of eight-hundred pounds a month had been halted.

Chapter 21

It wasn't too long ago that a criminal who could combine cleverness, imagination and freedom of movement had a good chance of staying out of prison. As he stepped across one country's border to enter another, he often left the irate police authorities helpless in his wake. There was very little the police could do, say in Peoria, Illinois, when the man they wanted was somewhere inside Asia.

Effective pursuit and eventual arrest of the international criminal are the result of good international police cooperation. This can be said to be the basic reason for Interpol's existence. The following case underscores the value of various police forces working in concert to apprehend a group of elusive and extremely capable criminals.

•

The man who arrived at the Gare du Nord in Paris to catch the afternoon train to Brussels looked like a high-salaried executive, which in a way, he was. He still had twenty minutes to spare when he hopped from the taxi in front of the station.

He stepped into the small money-exchange office just inside one of the entrances to the terminal, placed his expensive suitcase on the floor next to the counter, and presented the clerk with a hundred-dollar traveler's check drawn on a branch of the Bank of America in San Francisco.

For identification he offered a passport that showed him to be an American citizen named Frank Miller. He asked for French francs in return for the check and made a comment to the clerk that at the rate the dollar was falling, it would soon be two to one in relation to the franc. He spoke French with just enough of an accent to betray his American origins.

The clerk compared the signatures on the passport and the

174

check and counted out 410 francs for Frank Miller. Miller thanked him, pocketed his money, picked up his suitcase, and went to find his seat on the train.

Since he had a first-class ticket, he was not concerned with racing the mob of early summer tourists who were hurrying down the station platform. He knew most of them were traveling second class and would not be competing for a place with him.

He found two men, sitting next to the window, in his compartment. He hoisted his bag onto the rack over the seats, then sat down near the compartment door and lighted a cigarette. He wanted to use the three-hour trip to Brussels to get a little rest.

Miller was going to Belgium to take part in a business meeting with two of his associates. It was the first get-together the three of them had planned in more than three months. They had a lot to discuss. The three were involved in a business arrangement that was lucrative but risky. They had been conducting their affairs with good fortune for five months, and the meeting was to be used to consider some important changes.

•

As the train Frank Miller was on left the station, another American was standing in front of a police sergeant in a police station in Rome. This American was not resting. He was gesturing furiously at the calendar behind the officer's desk and asking him if he knew it was June 28.

It had been over one week, he said, since he had reported the loss of his wallet and personal papers to the police. What was taking them so long to recover the items?

The sergeant shrugged. He did not speak enough English to tell the man in front of him that they would probably never recover the things he had lost. The police received daily complaints of a similar nature. He managed to explain to the American that it would be better if he went to the American Embassy.

The American, whose Italian was as limited as the officer's

English, placed a business card on the desk. On it was scribbled his Rome hotel address. "If you find anything call me here," he said.

The policeman attached the card to the complaint form he had made out last week. The name on the card, like the one on the form, was Mark Burke. He felt sorry for the man. Not only had his passport been taken but also his reserve officer's identity card. Burke was a lieutenant commander in the Navy.

He assured Burke that he would certainly let him know at once if anything turned up.

•

When Frank Miller's train came into the Gare du Midi in Brussels, it was a little after six in the evening. He walked out into the lingering sunshine and took a taxi to the glass-fronted Hotel MacDonald. After checking in and being shown to his room, he went down to the Horseshoe Bar in the hotel and was immediately greeted by one of the men he had come to see, an Italian named Angelo Ori.

There was a marked contrast between the two men, even though both were wearing expensive and well-tailored clothes. Miller was tall and slender, with well-groomed, graying dark hair. He looked almost elegant.

Ori wore his clothes badly. He looked as if he had been sleeping in them. He was squat and short, with heavy square features and thinning black hair. He had a certain roughness of manner when he talked that clashed with the cultivated tones used by Miller.

Ori performed an important and necessary function in the three men's arrangement. Now he pointed to a brown attaché case at his feet and told Miller that inside the case there were ten new passports and six identity cards, including an American naval officer's I.D. card.

They ordered drinks, and as they were brought to them the third member of their group showed up. This was a German national, Otto Frenkel. Frenkel, too, performed an important function. He was a printer by profession and a good one. His specialty was producing false traveler's checks. As a sideline, he also altered stolen identity documents to fit Miller's needs.

He looked, except for having fairer skin and lighter hair, as if he could be Ori's twin brother. The resemblance was uncanny. He also had the same roughness of manner that was part of the Italian's personality.

The three of them spoke in English together. Frenkel told the other two that he had not come empty-handed to the meeting. He had brought some new passports for Miller and a quarter of a million dollars in forged traveler's checks. He explained, not without some pride, that the checks weren't from one bank but from several. It would make it a lot safer for Miller if he varied the checks when cashing them.

Ori brought up the fact that he had procured the naval officer's I.D. card. He wondered if it could be altered to suit Miller quickly. The normal procedure for the stolen identification that Ori delivered was for Frenkel to take it with him to his home in Munich and alter it at his leisure.

Frenkel said he would have to see it. If the photograph was at all close to Miller's looks, he might be able to smooth out the differences when he went back to his hotel room. Otherwise, he would have to take it home with him.

After they had all had a drink, they decided to continue their talk over dinner. They went to the Brussels Hilton to eat in the Maison de Boeuf restaurant.

During dinner, Miller said he thought a change of countries was in order. Europe had been worked too hard, it should be left alone for a while. He had cashed checks in every major European city during the past five months and he was sure the police had their eyes out for him. Miller suggested he try the Far East. It was virgin territory.

Ori didn't agree. He couldn't see the sense in finding a new place to do business when the old one had proven so successful. He asked why Miller was concerned. Wasn't he being supplied with frequent identity changes? How could they all coordinate if Miller went to Japan? He felt sure the police would never catch Miller in Europe.

Otto Frenkel sided with Miller. He thought they should let the European cities have a chance to cool off. By the time

Miller finished with a swing through the Orient, and then took a well-earned vacation, it would be possible to begin in Europe again. He thought Miller's idea excellent.

By the time the dinner was finished, the three had agreed that Miller would go to Japan next. They went back to Miller's hotel room, where Miller gave each of them a check for seventy-five thousand dollars' worth of Swiss francs drawn on a Zürich bank. The checks represented equal shares of the group's earnings since it went into business five months earlier. Like many legitimate businessmen, they kept a numbered Swiss bank account which they treated tenderly.

Before going their separate ways for the night, it was decided that upon Miller's return from the Far East, they would again meet in Brussels.

Brussels was a safe city for them. They made certain of that by never doing business in the city or for that matter anywhere in Belgium. To set the time for the next meeting they would use their established arrangement. Miller would send each man a coded telegram. The wording would indicate the time and date. The place would remain the same.

Miller stayed in Brussels over the weekend, then returned to Paris to catch his reserved flight to Japan. Naturally, his reservation on JAL Flight 672 was for a first-class passage.

Otto Frenkel returned to Munich before the weekend was over. He immediately started work on the new passports and identity cards supplied by Ori. The I.D. of the American officer was not with him. He had been able to take care of it before leaving Brussels, and it was now with Miller, along with the matching passport.

Ori, whose home was in Rome, decided to take a short holiday in Amsterdam before returning to Italy. He had no work to do. With the last batch of documents, the group had more than enough. He didn't have to worry about it anyway. In Rome, he had three men working for him stealing identification. He was certain that when he got back they would have some more for him.

Miller flew to Tokyo under the name of Stewart Jackson, using a United Kingdom passport. He was saving the American Navy identity of Mark Burke to use when cashing checks. It was part of a rule he had set for himself for safety. He never cashed checks with the identity he used for travel. There was always a small chance that information would get to the police before he got out of the country he was working. It would be more than embarrassing to be caught just because he was too careless to change documents.

In Tokyo, he found his hotel reservation confirmed and waiting in the Tokyo Hilton Hotel. He spent the first two days walking about the city. He had never been to Japan and was fascinated by what he saw. He was so fascinated that he spent still a third day looking around. However, he recovered quickly and went to work with a vengeance.

Using three different names, in five days he cashed twenty-six thousand dollars' worth of checks in Tokyo and Yokohama. Continuing his tour of Japan, he stopped off in Osaka, Kobe, Kyoto, and Nagoya, adding another seventeen thousand dollars to his profit.

He now returned to Tokyo and using three different banks had the money transferred to his Zürich bank. While doing this he used the name Alan Jason, the one listed with his numbered account in Switzerland.

From Tokyo, under the name Stewart Jackson, he took a midmorning JAL flight to Hong Kong. Arriving in the afternoon, he went at once to his hotel, the Mandarin. He was tired from his Japanese activities and slept for fifteen hours. As in Japan, he took a couple of days to explore the city before going to work. When he left Hong Kong on a flight for Singapore, he had enriched himself by eleven thousand more dollars.

While in Singapore for five days, he cashed eight thousand dollars in checks, took a quick trip into Malaysia, cashing five thousand dollars more, returned to Singapore in time to catch a plane to Bangkok, and gave himself a week's rest.

It was now time to set up the meeting in Brussels. He sent the coded telegrams to Ori and Frenkel on August 5, telling them to meet him in Brussels on August 9 at seven in the evening. In Bangkok, he had passed eight thousand dollars' worth of checks. It brought the total for the Asian tour to seventy-five thousand dollars.

When Otto Frenkel received the coded telegram he was relieved. He had expected to hear from Miller long before.

Now he hurriedly made preparations to leave his house in Munich. He had constructed a place in his cellar to hide his printing equipment and all the items connected with it. He had made a large hole in the floor into which he could lower the press by means of a hydraulic jack. It had taken him a lot of time and money to construct this hiding place, but he was not a man to spare expense where his safety was concerned.

It took him the best part of a morning to get everything in its place with a work table, draping a cloth over the table that trailed on the floor. He was ready to keep his appointment.

The telegram sent to Rome was not received by Angelo Ori. Ori was not in Rome, nor had he been during Miller's trip. He was still in Amsterdam, where he had met an Italian-speaking Danish tourist named Karen Jensen.

She was very impressed with Ori. He spent money as if he had millions and took her everywhere. She worked for a bank in Copenhagen and saved her money carefully each year for her vacations. According to what he had told her, he was a successful breeder of racehorses.

On the day that Angelo Ori should have been in Brussels he was thinking about going back to Copenhagen with her. She had only three more days of her vacation left. Ori proceeded to do something stupid. He confided in Karen Jensen. He explained why he had to go back to Rome. There might be a message already there for him, he said. He had been having such a good time with her that he had not been aware of the time passing.

He had not read Karen Jensen's character well. She was not impressed with what he told her. Rather she was shocked. She told him she would have to think about going to the police. It was a stupid thing for her to say.

Ori was standing in her hotel room. He grabbed her by the throat and started to strangle her. She wasn't strong and

180

quickly passed out from the pressure of his hands on her throat. He picked up a metal figurine from the night table and smashed it twice into her head. He left her in the room and ran from the hotel. He thought he had killed her and now wanted only to get back to Italy.

Chapter 22

For several months the General Secretariat of Interpol had been receiving complaints from various European countries that a well-organized group of criminals was passing forged traveler's checks in those countries. With the exception of Belgium and Switzerland, every nation in Europe had filed at least one complaint through its National Central Bureau.

The forged checks were not drawn on just one bank but on many. The printing work was exceptional. Even bank officials were unable to spot the checks as forgeries.

At first it appeared to be the work of a very large group of criminals. The signatures belonged to so many different people that the authorities felt a minimum of six persons had to be involved. Then, after the names on the checks had been investigated and it developed that all were those of people who had lost their personal identification, the police were able to judge that it was possible for just one or two men to be cashing the checks.

In addition, descriptions had been given the police by the banks and exchange offices where the checks were passed. Now the police could be certain only one man was responsible. But what a toll he took! In one five-day period, 283 forged checks had been passed in Vienna, Munich, and Stuttgart. In another six-day stretch, 347 checks had been passed in Paris, Lyon, Avignon, and Marseilles. Each of the checks was worth a hundred dollars. Spain fared no better. Barcelona, Valencia, Málaga, Córdoba, and Madrid accepted 257 of the forged traveler's checks.

Using the description of the man, the General Secretariat examined all of its specialized files for a clue to his identity. The photographic index, used in cases where no prints are available, was combed thoroughly and some copies of photos that came close to the description were sent to bank employees to see if they could make an identification.

The special file recording the actual offenses of criminals by type of offense, time, and place was thought to be a possible source for information. It was reasoned that the man they were looking for had probably been involved in the same type of thing before. But there was nothing in that file to help them.

Because Switzerland and Belgium were untouched, the searchers thought that the group might be headquartered in one of those two countries. The National Central Bureaus of Switzerland and Belgium were contacted and asked to see if they had anything in their records that might provide a lead. Neither country could come up with anything useful.

As the person cashing the checks never used a name he traveled under to cash a check, there was no way to find out what country he was in or had departed from. The investigation became extremely frustrating and, meanwhile, the checks continued to be cashed at an unbelievable rate.

One other possibility was explored. It was obvious that all the stolen identification had been acquired by people operating in Rome. With two exceptions, all the names on the checks were of visitors who had reported losing their documents in Italy, especially Rome. The police thought if they could pick up one of the persons stealing the identification, they might get a constructive lead.

The National Central Bureau of Italy was requested to begin a roundup of pickpockets, burglars, and known traffickers in false identification. Although many thieves of this type were questioned, none of them could give any positive information to the police.

Then, quite suddenly, all activity of the mysterious check passer ceased. The police were puzzled, then pleased. If nothing else, at least money losses were halted.

Interpol, of course, had not given up on the case. They continued transferring information to the various National Central Bureaus and continued to compile a file on the unknown criminal.

In the middle of July, complaints began again, this time from the Far East. Interpol quickly recognized the method used. It was their man again, working in a new territory. The police in that part of the world were just as baffled as their counterparts in Europe. They were helpless. It was a case of too many name changes, too many countries hit. In spite of the fact that the police authorities of the entire world were joined in the hunt, the wanted man was still very much at large and very much in operation.

Then, the General Secretariat got some information on the case from Amsterdam. The police there had questioned a victim of an attempted murder, a Danish tourist, Karen Jensen. She had told them what she knew about Angelo Ori, and the facts seemed to tie in with the forged checks. She had no idea where Ori was but knew he lived somewhere in Rome and had said he needed to go there to see if a message was waiting for him.

Karen Jensen had spent five days in an intensive-care unit. The police hadn't been able to question her until she was out of danger.

Interpol-Italy was asked to locate Ori. The Italian police were able to supply the General Secretariat with Ori's photograph, fingerprints, and arrest and prison record.

A red notice was immediately issued by the General Secretariat. Included was an arrest warrant for attempted murder. The Dutch wanted to extradite Ori as soon as he could be found.

It didn't take long to pick him up. He was arrested in Lisbon on the night of August 17. He was traveling under the name Antonio Gomes, but the red notice had done its job.

Ori didn't try to fight extradition. Taken to Amsterdam, he was confronted by Karen Jensen, and she made a positive identification of him as her attacker. He was formally charged with attempted murder and locked up.

Because of his suspected connection with the checks, Ori was questioned vigorously by the police. He didn't say too much for a while. He admitted that he did supply the identification used, and that he had made a lot of money during the operation. He also told about the coded telegram that had been waiting for him in Rome. He said that after leaving Amsterdam he had gone back to Rome, seen the telegram, realized he had missed the Brussels meeting, and then gone to Lisbon. He knew the police would be looking for him because of what he had tried to do to Karen Jensen. Even if Karen was dead, he was sure someone would be able to identify him since he had spent so much time with her in Amsterdam.

The police asked him about his two partners, but at first Ori refused to talk about them. He told the police he had a sense of honor and would accept any punishment coming to him, but under no circumstances would he implicate the other two men.

Then, after three more days of questioning, Ori changed his mind. He told the police that one of the men was Otto Frenkel, from Munich. The other man, the one cashing the checks and the ringleader, he knew only as Alan Jason. He wasn't sure if that was really the man's name, but it had been on a check from a Zürich bank.

This information was given to the General Secretariat and to Federal Germany's National Central Bureau in Wiesbaden. Frenkel was picked up at his home on August 23. Despite all the precautions he had taken to hide his printing equipment, the police found it the same day.

By the following day, Frenkel had given the police a lot of information. He explained how he had gotten together with the man known to him as Alan Jason. They had met in Rome, and after they had agreed to go into business, Jason had found Ori. He didn't know the connection between the two men. He was a printer, and only that, he explained to the police. He wanted to know what they thought of his checks.

The police thought he must know more about Jason. It didn't seem possible that both Frenkel and Ori knew virtually nothing about Jason. However, continued questioning of both men provided no further information.

The Zürich bank was located with the help of the Swiss National Central Bureau but could only say that the money had been withdrawn from Jason's account a few days earlier.

The search for Alan Jason got underway. The General Secretariat circulated a list of all the known aliases Jason used and his description. The circulars were sent to each of Interpol's member nations.

A month went by. Still there was nothing on the elusive Jason. Then, toward the end of October, a complaint about a forged traveler's check drawn on the Bank of America and signed by a man calling himself Mark Burke was reported by the National Central Bureau of Lebanon. The man had used an identity card showing him to be a reserve officer in the United States Navy.

The United States Treasury Department was contacted and soon replied that the name and rank did not belong to the man who had cashed the check. They knew this because the real Mark Burke was in Denver, Colorado, in a Veterans' Administration Hospital, where he had undergone surgery on the same day the check was passed in Beirut. They were also able to supply the facts about Burke's loss of his personal identification in Rome.

The National Central Bureau of the Netherlands asked Angelo Ori if he remembered a passport and identity card belonging to Burke. He said he couldn't be sure, he had had too many in his hands to remember one in particular. Ori, by now, had been sentenced to three years' imprisonment for his attack on Karen Jensen. He had just begun to serve his sentence.

Otto Frenkel, resting in a German prison, was able to tell the police that he thought he had worked on the Burke identity when the three men met in Brussels in late June. But he also wasn't certain.

The police were right back where they had started. The name Alan Jason had proved to be as spurious as the other names used by the wanted man. It belonged to a deceased Canadian.

•

The police weren't the only ones with problems. The object of their search was beginning to have a few of his own.

186

He had run out of false identities and at last was using his real name and passport. Under this name, George Turner, he checked into the Hotel Kent in Ankara, Turkey. It wasn't a wise choice, considering his American passport. Political tensions were rising because of the Cyprus situation, and Americans were rapidly becoming unpopular in Turkey.

Turner didn't know that Otto Frenkel and Angelo Ori had been arrested. It probably wouldn't have bothered him if he had known. He had broken up his arrangements with those two when Ori failed to appear for the Brussels meeting on August 9. He had told Frenkel at that time that he was getting out. If Ori was under arrest, it would not be long before the police would be looking for them. Frenkel had agreed with him.

After leaving Brussels, Turner had gone to Zürich and closed out his account in the bank. From there, using aliases supplied by Frenkel, he had gone to Lisbon, then London, then Cairo, then to Beirut, where he had cashed one check under the name of Burke, and finally to Ankara.

He wasn't sure what he wanted to do next. He had chosen Ankara simply because he'd never been there and felt he'd like to take a look at Turkey.

On the third of December, Turner was arrested by the Turkish Police. He was charged with consorting with a Greek spy. It had come about in this way. Turner had met a man of Turkish nationality but Greek parentage, named Dimitrios Constantimos. Constantimos was suspected of political action detrimental to the Turkish government, and it was known that he had family in the Greek part of Cyprus.

Turner had spent several evenings in this man's company, and they had discussed the Turkish invasion of Cyprus. They had been overheard by a minor government official who reported their conversation. The next time they discussed Cyprus they were heard again, this time by two military investigators.

The authorities decided to arrest Turner and find out what his business was in Turkey. During the questioning that followed his arrest, it soon became obvious to the police that he had no political intentions in Ankara. However, as part of their investigation they inspected all of his personal belongings. They found several false passports and a large sum of money. They asked Turner about this, and he was unable to give a satisfactory reply.

He was now turned over to the National Central Bureau of Turkey, which made contact with both the National Central Bureau of the United States and the General Secretariat.

Things began to move rapidly. The Americans said that they had no special information about Turner. His passport was legitimate and had been issued in San Francisco in November 1973.

The General Secretariat, however, was very interested to learn that among the passports discovered in Turner's belongings was one in the name of Mark Burke and one in the name of Alan Jason. They had found their man at long last.

Extradition requests began to come into Ankara from almost every city in Europe and the Far East. Sixteen countries wanted him, wanted him enough to start extradition proceedings. There were several countries that didn't bother.

Lebanon was the first to place Turner on trial. He was sentenced to one year in prison, early in 1975. When he is released, seven countries will contest with each other for the right to extradite him next.

Otto Frenkel and Angelo Ori, whose looks resemble one another, also have a similarity in the number of holds placed against them by different countries. They too have more than a few court appearances waiting for them when they are released from prison.

Chapter 23

According to information on file at the General Secretariat of Interpol, most girls who are forced into prostitution have an idea of what will be expected of them when they accept recruitment for jobs abroad as "ballet dancers" or "entertainers." The prospect of making money quickly is the motivating factor for them. What they don't seem to realize, at least in certain cases, is the fact they will be forced to work night and day, be kept in short supply of money, and lose their freedom as well. It is often too late when they find this out.

There are instances, however, when the standard form of recruitment is not used. Some girls are forced into prostitution after being abducted. This is rare, but it does happen, usually with very young girls.

•

Professor Richard Whitman, his wife Mildred, and their two daughters had come down to the last four days of a four-week vacation in Istanbul during the summer of 1973. Whitman, who taught philosophy at the University of London, had thought it was a good idea to bring the girls, Elaine, aged thirteen, and Jennifer, aged twelve, on the holiday. He'd explained to his wife that it was an excellent opportunity for the children to see something of the world and absorb a different culture. His wife had not been in favor of their coming along. She thought they were too young to appreciate what they would see and felt the extra expenses involved would prove unwarranted.

During the time the family spent in Istanbul they had methodically taken in the main tourist attractions, allotting a set period of the day for each site. It was done according to a plan devised by Whitman. A very methodical type, he had each day worked out in a little notebook which he carried with him.

The two girls objected to this way of seeing the city. What they most strenuously objected to was the daily nap that all the family took between the hours of two and five in the afternoon. Whitman explained that it was an important part of the day because it gave them a chance to rest and also was in keeping with Turkish custom.

Perhaps because of the disciplined days, a lot of friction developed among the four of them. Whitman was adamant about his daily planning, and Mildred was placed in the role of keeping peace between father and children.

Elaine and Jennifer shared a room adjoining their parents' room on the second floor of the Divan Oteli, a hotel not far from the Hilton on Cumhuriyet Caddesi Harbiye. On August 22, a Thursday, the girls rebelled against the afternoon nap.

While Richard and Mildred Whitman dutifully slept, Elaine and Jennifer slipped from their room, raced down the hotel stairway, ran through the lobby and out into the bright afternoon sun. They wanted, just once, to see the streets and shops of Istanbul without the close supervision of their parents. They had no definite plans except to take the first city bus they saw and ride on it until they came to any interesting place where they could get off and walk around. It would be easy to get back. All they needed to do was remember the number of the bus and, if an emergency arose, they could always take a taxi.

·

Ekrem Ozturk was the owner of a night club located close to the point where the Galata Bridge spanned the Golden Horn. The club was on the side of the river that also housed such historical treasures as the Topkapi Palace, the Blue Mosque, and St. Sophia.

The night club, called the Kismet, featured belly dancers and watered-down liquor. The belly dancers doubled as prostitutes. Customers of the club were mainly rich Turks who came to buy the services of the prostitutes and mix with an element of criminals who used the club as a regular meeting place.

Ozturk had the reputation of being able to supply a girl to fit the taste of any man. The price was high, but his regular clients could afford it. It was even rumored that if a customer wished to spend enough money, Ozturk would provide him with a virgin. The Turkish Police believed that Ozturk was also engaged in transportation of girls to other countries and kept him under intermittent surveillance.

It was, naturally, not without pleasure that Ozturk gazed at the two young girl tourists who were standing in front of the closed doors of his club in the midafternoon sun and who were so obviously lost.

Elaine, speaking slowly and loudly, as she had watched her father do when speaking to foreigners, asked if Ozturk knew of a place that had a clean public toilet.

Ozturk, who spoke English reasonably well if not fluently, observed the two girls for a moment without saying anything. They were both blond, slim, and leggy, with blue eyes and turned-up noses. He knew at once they were sisters.

"Are you lost?" he asked.

Elaine's impression of Ozturk was that he was a very large and very dirty-looking man who perspired a lot. Jennifer thought he looked fierce, with his swarthy skin and mustache curling down to the corners of his mouth, but she felt he was pleasant in manner. She wasn't as fastidious as her sister.

Elaine admitted that they were lost.

Ozturk asked what hotel they were staying at. He would be happy to direct them to it, he explained.

Elaine thanked him but told him that at the moment it was more important to find a toilet than to find their hotel. She tugged at Jennifer's hand to urge her to move along.

Ozturk told them that he owned the club they were standing in front of and would be happy to unlock the door to let the girls use the toilet inside. Before they could make up their minds to accept his offer, he had opened the door and motioned them in.

He told them the toilets were at the rear of the club,

pointing in that direction. It was dark, and Ozturk switched on some of the lights which illuminated the Kismet.

When the girls were ready to leave, Ozturk asked them if they wanted a cold drink. He could give them some lemonade if they wished, he said.

The girls accepted eagerly, and while they had their drinks, Ozturk asked them a lot of questions about their family and what they were doing in Turkey and how they liked his country.

They answered politely, taking care not to say anything that might offend him. They had been repeatedly instructed by their parents to be careful about mentioning things to strangers that could be construed as offensive. As a matter of fact, although the girls had enjoyed seeing Istanbul, they much preferred to spend the summer holidays with their friends at the beach in England.

When they had finished their drinks, Ozturk offered them another but they refused politely, explaining they had to get started back to the hotel. They wanted to be sure to be back before five.

"Don't worry," Ozturk said. "I'll drive you to your hotel."

The girls said it wasn't necessary. They could get back by themselves if he would only give them directions to a bus.

Ozturk insisted on taking them home. He had two little girls himself, he said, about their age. He would like to think an English father would do the same for them if they were lost in London. He poured them some more lemonade and told them he would get his car from the garage. He would be back in a few minutes and meanwhile they could enjoy their drinks.

Ten minutes passed and Ozturk had not returned. The two girls began to get uneasy, alone in the club, which seemed very large with the empty tables and open dance floor. Elaine suggested that they leave. After all, she said, they had no real obligation to remain, and besides, they would never see the man again.

Even as she said this, the door opened and Ozturk

reappeared. He had someone else with him, a small dark man dressed in a wrinkled suit.

The girls said they were ready to leave. They didn't like the way the small dark man stared at them. As Elaine and Jennifer moved toward the door, the small man blocked their way.

In very good English he asked if they would like a tour of Istanbul. They explained they had already seen Istanbul with their parents.

Ozturk now offered them another drink. This frightened the girls. It was obvious to them now that the two men were trying to keep them with them. Elaine said loudly that it was high time she and her sister were on their way to their hotel.

The men exchanged some words in Turkish and then Ozturk asked Elaine if she had ever seen a real Turkish nightclub show. He told her he was inviting them for dinner and the show that evening. It would be a new and interesting experience for them, he promised.

"We can't," Elaine said. Once more she explained that their parents were expecting them no later than five and that it was very necessary that they get going at once. If they didn't get back, she said pointedly, her parents would no doubt call the police.

Ozturk scowled. He spoke again to the other man in Turkish. When he stopped speaking, with a quick look at the small man, he grabbed Elaine around the waist and scooped her up under his arm. At the same time, the small man grabbed Jennifer by the right arm and began to push her toward the rear of the club in the direction of the toilets. Ozturk followed, carrying Elaine.

The girls screamed but were unable to free themselves. The small man pushed open a door and switched on a light that exposed a narrow staircase leading down under the club. The girls were carried down the stairs and into another small room, where they were tied and gagged. Ozturk made sure the ropes tying them back to back were secure, then, with a shrug at the other man, gestured for him to follow him from the

193

room. A second later the light in the room went out, leaving the two girls alone with the darkness.

•

Mildred Whitman awoke just in time to shut off the alarm on the little travel clock before it rang at five o'clock. She hated having to live by an alarm on vacation, but it was part of her husband's program. The best she could do was to wake early and turn the alarm off. She nudged her husband out of his sleep and went to waken the girls. It was time for them to get up too.

Mrs. Whitman was surprised to discover the girls' room empty when she entered it. A glance at the beds told her they hadn't been used. She called out the information to her husband, who was sitting on the edge of his bed. He came into the room with an exasperated look.

His wife was secretly a little pleased. She was sure the girls had gotten tired of the regimen imposed by her husband. Even if she didn't have the nerve to rebel, evidently the girls had, and were out doing some independent sightseeing. She was sure they would be back shortly and said so.

"I don't like it," Whitman said. He always got upset if his orderly plans went astray. The fact that the girls were not in their room upset him greatly.

His wife pointed out that they might just have gone down to the lobby to get a cold drink. She suggested that he call the desk clerk and ask if the girls were in the lobby.

Whitman called and was told the girls had left the hotel a little after two. They had not returned, the clerk informed Whitman.

Whitman put the phone down in a very bad humor. He raged to his wife about how dangerous it was for two young girls to be running around a city where they didn't speak the language. When they returned, he said, he would discipline them severely.

"Why don't we wait a little while before we get all upset?" his wife asked. She knew that her husband tended to be an alarmist. An hour later she was more nevous than he.

194

"What do we do now?" she asked.

"Wait," Whitman said. He again told her that he would punish them for this stunt.

His wife thought they should not waste any more time before calling the police.

Whitman said he thought that was an idiotic idea. What did she imagine the police would think if he called and said his daughters were an hour late? They would laugh and dismiss him as a crazy father, that's all.

Mildred said she didn't mind being laughed at. The girls might have taken off to have private look at the city, but they were obedient girls and would have been back by now if everything was all right. She was sure something had happened to them. She again asked Whitman to call the police or, if he wouldn't do that, to call the British Embassy.

Whitman refused. He insisted they wait one more hour. Suppose the girls had simply gotten lost, and that was all. How stupid they would look if they began making calls all over the place for no good reason. No, they would wait another hour before taking any action. He was sure the girls would return within that time.

Gradually, as the minutes passed, the father's anger turned to deep concern. Whitman, who had been pacing the floor, turned to his wife after three quarters of an hour and told her he wasn't waiting any longer. He picked up the phone, got the desk clerk, and told him his daughters were missing and that he wanted the police.

At exactly seven-thirty, there was a knock on the Whitmans' hotel-room door. He opened it, hoping to see his girls, but two men were standing there with serious looks on their faces.

They introduced themselves as detectives from the Turkish Police. They had come as quickly as they could, they explained, and the small delay was due to having to find detectives who spoke English.

The Whitmans told them what they knew, chiefly that the two girls had left the hotel during the time set aside for an afternoon nap and had not yet returned.

The detectives asked for the girls' passports. They would need them for identification and also to make copies of the photographs to circulate among the police.

"You make it sound as if it could take a long time to find them." Mildred Whitman said.

One of the detectives nodded. "Istanbul is a big city."

Chapter 24

Richard Whitman had been quite wrong. The police had no intention of laughing at him, nor would they have if he had reported his daughters missing at the time his wife first suggested he do so.

The many stories about Istanbul being a dangerous place for unescorted girls had a basis in fact. It was not unheard of for girl tourists to be abducted on the streets, and their age was not necessarily any protection.

One of the two detectives who came to see the Whitmans, Inspector Hamza Hoyuk, promptly initiated two levels of police action. First was the normal check of all hospitals and police posts in the city to see if the girls had turned up at any of them. He didn't expect much from that quarter. Even if there had been an accident, it was unlikely that both girls were so critically injured that they would be incapable of contacting their parents, and if the police picked them up for some reason, they would already have been returned to the hotel.

The second thing Inspector Hoyuk did was to have copies made of the passport photographs for immediate distribution to all the police stations. If, as he already suspected, the girls were victims of an abduction, the police had to act with the utmost speed. He had reached the conclusion that they were dealing with an abduction because it was the only conclusion that made sense to him. They were too young to be carrying enough money to make robbery worthwhile, and killing two young girls just for the sake of killing them didn't make much sense either. That left abduction. He didn't have to think about the purpose.

Because Hoyuk was an experienced police officer he tried to cover every contingency. There was a good chance that an attempt might be made to slip the girls out of Turkey. If that were to occur, more than the Turkish Police would be needed. Without hesitation, he called the National Central Bureau of Turkey and explained the situation to them. He also had copies of the girls' photographs sent to them at once so they could transmit them to the General Secretariat for worldwide distribution.

If the kidnappers worked rapidly and got the girls out of the country, they would have to bring them in through some other country's entry point. Hoyuk wanted to be certain that when they did try to cross a border with the girls the police would be waiting.

Meanwhile, he himself would lead the hunt in Istanbul. He made arrangements to have roadblocks set up at once. The airport, railroad terminals, and harbors on the Anatolian shore would be alerted as well. When he had finished with all this it was still not quite ten o'clock.

Hoyuk now issued orders to have police investigate all the clubs known to use prostitutes as well as those places known to be hangouts for criminals. It was a lot of ground to cover and would take many men, but Hoyuk had been given a free hand by his superiors to proceed with the search.

•

Ekrem Oztruk sipped a drink at one of the tables in his crowded club. He had a meeting scheduled at ten o'clock with an Italian national, Mario Diletti. Diletti owned a similar type of club in Naples and was in Istanbul looking for prostitutes. He had done business with Oztruk twice before and had purchased a total of five girls from the owner of the Kismet.

It was almost ten and Ozturk wanted to get his deal with Diletti finished quickly because he had another customer arriving sometime later. This other customer was from Ankara, where he did a big business in drugs and prostitutes. He had been contacted earlier in the day by Ozturk and told that there were two young English girls for sale. He had told Ozturk he had other business to complete in Istanbul but would stop by the Kismet for a look at the merchandise before the night was over.

198

Diletti showed up exactly at ten and entered at once into conversation with Ozturk, ignoring the sweaty, heavy-breasted dancers gyrating on the floor. He made arrangements to buy five girls from Ozturk. They shook hands on the deal after agreeing on the price, and Diletti rose to leave.

Ozturk asked him at this point if he would be interested in buying two very young English girls. In reply to the Italian's question as to how old they were, Ozturk said he thought about twelve or thirteen. At this Diletti laughed and said he was sure Ozturk was joking. The Turk assured him it wasn't a joke. If Diletti wanted to see for himself, Ozturk would be happy to show him the girls. Diletti said he wasn't interested anyway. What he wanted, he had brought—girls old enough to do what they were supposed to without urging.

A few minutes after Diletti left the club, the small dark man who'd helped Ozturk seize the girls arrived at the table. He worked for Ozturk in the capacity of club manager. His name was Sadan Alkim. With him was another man, the man interested in looking at the girls. He was known to Ozturk and Alkim only by the name of Afif.

The three of them went down to the basement room where the girls were being held. Ozturk explained it was a safe place to keep them because it was practically soundproof. He'd originally had it built as a storage room but on occasion found other uses for it.

Ozturk opened the door to the room and switched on a light. The two girls were in the same position they had been tied, back to back. They turned their heads to look at the men with tear-streaked faces and fear in their eyes.

Afif grunted and said something to Ozturk in Turkish. Ozturk and Alkim moved to the girls and undid the rope holding them together. Holding each girl by the shoulders the men brought them to their feet. Because of the gags they couldn't talk, but the sobbing sounds coming from their throats were audible.

Afif came close to them and looked them over. He reached out one hand and patted Elaine on the top of the head, then repeated the motion with Jennifer. He said something in

Turkish that made both Ozturk and Alkim chuckle, then bending down ran his hands up Elaine's legs, stroking the skin. She tried to squirm away but couldn't move in Ozturk's grip.

Afif continued to inspect the girls as if he were inspecting livestock. Ozturk and Alkim held them still while Afif completed his examination. When he was finished, he grunted at Ozturk, and the girls were once more tied back to back on the floor.

Upstairs, seated at a table in the club, they got down to the business of price. Ozturk wanted five thousand American dollars for the two of them. Afif was willing to pay three thousand. The only way he would consider five, he said to Ozturk, was if he were permitted to try them out before he bought them.

To this, Ozturk flatly refused. How could he be sure, he wanted to know, that Afif would decide he wanted them after trying them? If Afif changed his mind, he, Ozturk, would be left with damaged merchandise. Virgins brought a premium price, he stated, and he was sure these two were virgins. If Afif wasn't interested, he was sure he could find another buyer. Afif said he would think it over and let Ozturk know by morning. He had a drink, then left the club.

•

Police, checking out clubs where prostitution was known be part of the entertainment, walked into the Kismet at eleven-thirty. They were in uniform and were greeted cordially by the employees. Ozturk came over to speak to them and offered them drinks, which they refused.

They asked if he had heard anything about two English girls being abducted. Ozturk said he was surprised they would ask him such a question. They knew he ran an honest business and didn't deal in abductions.

He was told that if he heard anything he had better contact the police at once. They weren't fooling around about this search for the two girls. Anyone who had knowledge and kept it back would be dealt with harshly.

When they left, Ozturk had a hurried conference with

Alkim. They decided they had better get rid of the girls as soon as they could. Evidently the police were hot and there would be a lot of trouble ahead. Ozturk called Afif at the number he had been given and told him he had reconsidered and would accept three thousand provided Afif made arrangements to pick up the girls that night.

Afif told him it would take a little time to make the arrangements but that he would stop by with the money and everything ready to take possession of the girls before two in the morning, when the club officially closed.

·

Mario Diletti had run into grief a few minutes before the police walked into the Kismet. He had been picked up in a club that catered to racketeer types, where he had just been invited to sit down to discuss some business with three men known to the Turkish Police as pimps who worked the tourist hotels.

Diletti claimed to be a tourist who had wandered into the club. His Turkish was weak, and the policemen's Italian was nonexistent. Because of the people with him, he was brought into police headquarters for further questioning.

At ten minutes after midnight, Inspector Hoyuk, still covering every possible chance, requested Interpol-Turkey to telex Interpol-Italy under a high-priority code for specific information on Diletti.

The telexed answer was relayed to Hoyuk at five minutes to one. Diletti was known to the Italian police as a constant offender of prostitution laws. He was also the owner of a club in Naples that specialized in prostitutes.

Hoyuk decided to question Diletti personally. He had an interpreter brought to his office and began his questioning at one-thirty.

With Diletti sitting in a chair across from his desk, Hoyuk wasted no time. He explained that he knew who Diletti was and what he suspected Diletti was doing in Istanbul. He said that the police were searching for two English girls and that he thought Diletti might have talked to someone who knew something about it. He was willing, he said, to let Diletti walk out the door if the Italian could supply him with any useful information.

Diletti took about ten seconds to think over the deal. He said he had been offered two young English girls for sale by a man he knew slightly, the owner of the Kismet club, Ekrem Ozturk.

At ten minutes to two, Hoyuk and three plainclothes detectives entered the Kismet. Outside the club, two carloads of policemen had stationed themselves at points to cover every exit. They had orders to see that no one left the club until Hoyuk said it was all right.

Alkim met the detectives at the door and told them they were a little late. The club was due to close in ten minutes, and unfortunately they weren't allowing any more guests inside. Perhaps the group would like to come back the following night?

Hoyuk identified himself and demanded to speak to Ozturk. Alkim suggested he should go to find his boss, but the inspector said it would be better if Alkim remained with the policemen. Then Ozturk, spotting the new arrivals, came over.

He recognized one of the detectives and tried to play the role of the hearty host. Hoyuk cut him short and told him he had reason to believe that the two girls were somewhere in the club.

Ozturk responded to this with outrage. He knew nothing, he said, about any English girls. The police had been in earlier that evening asking the same questions. He had told them, as he was now telling Hoyuk, that if he heard anything he would report it. If the detectives didn't believe him, they should feel free to search the club. He had nothing to hide.

Hoyuk had three more policemen come into the club. He ordered two of them to keep Alkim and Ozturk under guard, then he had the house lights turned up. He announced that everyone should remain in his place. As he finished speaking one of his men came in from the street pushing the man known as Afif in front of him.

"He tried to run away when he saw us," the policeman told Hoyuk.

Hoyuk ordered Afif held along with Ozturk and Alkim. Then he and another detective began a systematic search of the club. It didn't take long to discover the door leading to the basement. Hoyuk descended the stairs and looked around. There wasn't much to see except cases of liquor and some loose planks of wood.

A stack of empty cardboard cartons caught his eye. There was something strange about them, and as he approached he saw what it was. They were completely out of place with the rest of the surroundings. Everything else was just tossed about at random. These cartons were carefully stacked against the wall and, although they were heavily coated with dust, there were very visible fingerprints showing where they had been lifted into their present position. Hoyuk pushed at the center of the stack, and the cartons tumbled to the floor. He was now looking at a door. He tried the handle but it was locked. He put his ear against the door but could hear nothing.

Hoyuk called to his man at the top of the stairs to bring Ozturk. When the owner of the club came down the stairs, Hoyuk pointed at the door. "Open it."

"I can't," Ozturk said. He explained that the door had been locked for years. He had never known what was behind it.

Hoyuk ordered Ozturk to empty his pockets. When a set of keys appeared, Hoyuk told him it would be easier if he admitted which key opened the door. Sooner or later the door would be opened, Hoyuk said, even if he finally had to break it down.

At this Ozturk pointed to a key. Hoyuk inserted it into the lock and turned the handle. The door swung open and from the basement light the huddled figures of the two girls could clearly be seen.

•

Ekrem Ozturk, Sadan Alkim, and the man known as Afif, whose full name was Afif Icmeli, were charged with kidnapping, Afif as an accessory to the crime. They were convicted and sentenced to prison.

Mario Diletti was released from custody but told to leave the county. He is forbidden to enter Turkey again.

The two girls were returned, unharmed, to their parents.

•

It would be impossible to list every case in which direct or indirect intervention by Interpol has been the deciding factor. In many of the cases, Interpol has participted to the extent of a single message or piece of information. Perhaps the case would have been closed without Interpol's aid. Sometimes it's difficult to say.

What is not difficult to say is that Interpol has made it possible for the police of all nations to coordinate their efforts and cooperate with each other effectively.